WHAT OTHERS ARE SAYING ABOUT *TEN WAYS TO PRAY*

"Harrell's book is a masterful intersection of devotion and scholarship. Rich in inspiration, practical and adaptable for both individuals and small groups, there is something here for believers in any tradition or at any stage of their Christian pilgrimage. The ten models for prayer she has culled from church history and its two millennia of practice and tradition are beautifully woven together with short biographical sketches of the pioneers of the faith who are most closely associated with them. Harrell offers bountiful and insightful suggestions on how Christians in the twenty-first century will benefit and be blessed by incorporating facets of these prayers as part of their daily walk, as well as in longer seasons of prayer or retreat. Questions for contemplation, application and/or discussion with others, detailed study notes, and extensive bibliographies make this small volume an invaluable addition to any believer's arsenal of devotional aids."—*Thomas Crumb, Pastor, First Congregational Church of Pomfret, Pomfret Center, Connecticut*

"*Ten Ways to Pray* celebrates the gift of prayer. Here readers are invited to explore their relationships with God and to learn to pray. It is a valuable resource for teachers, students, spiritual directors, and anyone desirous of deepening their spiritual life. This very readable and practical book provides a history of each type of prayer and the practice of the prayer for both individuals and groups. I highly recommend it."—*Kathleen Hagerty, Spiritual Director and Interfaith Chaplain, Solomon Carter Fuller Mental Health Center, Boston, Massachusetts*

"Dawn Duncan Harrell has captured the attention and interest of the reader by presenting several disciplines of prayer for all who yearn to go deeper in their relationships with Christ, to listen and hear his voice, and to respond to his leading. The use of story-telling, centered around ten faithful Christians, gives the reader an informative snapshot of why the particular method was practiced. *Ten Ways to Pray* is a powerful tool for personal use or within the small group venue. The reflection and personal questions are well-constructed and, without a doubt, create edifying dialogue. This book will certainly awaken the reader to a new level of experiencing the power of prayer!" —*Diana Curren Bennett, Director of Spiritual Leadership Communities and Consultant for Small Group Ministry, Leadership Transformations, Inc., Director of Small Group Ministries, Christ Chapel, Centerville, Massachusetts*

TEN WAYS
TO PRAY

TEN WAYS
TO PRAY

A SHORT GUIDE TO A LONG HISTORY
OF TALKING WITH GOD

Dawn Duncan Harrell

for Marcia Duncan, who seeks the one thing,
and for Steve Duncan, who eagerly inquires,
and for their granddaughter Violet

One thing have I asked of the Lord, that will I seek after; that I may dwell in the house of the Lord all the days of my life, to behold the beauty of the Lord, and to inquire in his temple.—Psalm 27:4

Contents

Introduction
HABITS OF PRAYER

Fostering Prayer

"The problem with classes on prayer is that you spend most of the time talking about prayer and very little time praying," my husband complained.

At dinner, my sister had explained her frustrations in preparing such a class for her church's adult education slot. The rest of us were pulling easier-said-than-done pins and lobbing suggestion like small grenades. "Just teach what Jesus did," my father repeated. "You can't go wrong with the Lord's Prayer."

"OK. But we need to offer a few steps," she reasoned. "Jesus walked on water two verses after he prayed (Mark 6:46, 48), but the rest of us get discouraged with goals like that."

She had already read many helpful books. She found giants of the faith such as E. M. Bounds, Ole Hallesby, Andrew Murray, Watchman Nee, Charles Spurgeon, and R. A. Torrey quoted frequently. More modern authors such as Jill Briscoe, Richard Foster, Stanley Grenz, Margaret Guenther, Abraham Heschel, Peter Kreeft, and Thomas Merton offered thoughtful encouragement, descriptions, histories, and theologies of prayer. Best-sellers such as David Yonggi Cho, Stormie O'Martian, and Dutch Sheets advocated intercessory prayer and told countless anecdotes to inspire confidence that prayer *is* powerful and it *does* work. Philip Yancey reported on prayer. Bill Hybels and

John White lead readers through studies and meditations. She herself preferred to use the Puritan and Celtic prayers that were recorded by Arthur Bennett and the Northumbria Community, or the ancient devotional writings that Emilie Griffin, James Bryan Smith, and Phyllis Tickle had gathered.

However, while these authors wrote *about prayer,* she wanted her class *to pray.*

I pulled my pin and tossed. "Give a five-minute history on one type of prayer that the church has practiced, boil it down into practical 'how-tos,' and then practice it. Try another kind the next week."

Practicing actual prayer is by far the most important aim of this book. In *Prayer: The Cry for the Kingdom,* Stanley Grenz notes, "Prayer, it would seem, is not a topic to be discussed but a task to be done."[1] Hearing God and feeling heard by him satisfies a deep hunger in our souls. Studying how to do that can only go so far. Being inspired by others' experiences can only go so far. Recognizing our place in the history of God's praying people fulfills only a portion of the process. We must also join with them in seeking the Lord and thinking his thoughts after him (Isa 55:6–9). We must actually spend time with God if we want to develop our own conversations with him. To quote my dad again, we must "*Do* something!" We must pray.

Still, Grenz goes on to write, "Praying well requires that we be taught to pray."[2] Knowing how helps us get started.

---

[1] Stanley Grenz, *Prayer: The Cry for the Kingdom* (rev. ed.; Grand Rapids, Mich.: Eerdmans, 2005), 6.
[2] Ibid., 7.

Learning different ways to listen deepens the habit or loosens us from a rut. And considering others' stories encourages us to keep trying.

Joining the Faithful Communion

Do you need to start or re-energize a habit of prayer? In each of the following chapters, we will learn a historical method of praying. And then practice it. Find an approach that works for you. Study alone or with your spiritual friend or small group. Read the book from front to back or dip into chapters that catch your interest.

Every chapter introduces one of our forebears in his or her struggle to connect with God and a type of prayer he or she favored. Richard Foster encourages us to listen to them. "We are helped immensely by looking at their efforts and learning their stories," he writes in *Streams of Living Water*. "Furthermore, it is a genuine act of humility to realize that we can learn from others who have gone before us. To be sure, they made mistakes, but even so they have much to teach us."[3] Their histories are worth considering because they tell about God's communication with his people. In turn, our praying sisters and brothers can help us to discover and feel known by our Creator.

I learned about God at the knees of my own parents and grandparents and by watching others in the churches I have attended. Yet even the church history class I took in

---

[3] Richard J. Foster, *Streams of Living Water: Celebrating the Great Traditions of Christian Faith* (New York: HarperSanFrancisco, 1998), 22.

graduate school quickly demonstrated that my family tree of prayer stretches back still further.

Breath prayer, the first of ten methods we will explore, is a good example. Its current popularity began at the turn of the twentieth century as it emerged from Russian Orthodox monasteries and entered the spiritual disciplines of the West. But the custom is far older than that. Through the Eastern Orthodox Church, it can be traced back to the split between Eastern and Western Churches in the Middle Ages and from there to early church fathers of the fourth century such as Gregory of Nyssa.

Similarly, the chapters in this book are arranged in reverse chronological order, beginning with several nineteenth century saints, covering the Reformation and Roman Catholic Counter-Reformation, and concluding with Benedict and Gregory of Nyssa of the fifth and fourth centuries respectively.

In each chapter, a section entitled "Practice" follows the story with several steps for trying the method. If your time is too short for a practice session, "Sample the Prayer" offers suggestions for how to incorporate the method into your day or week. Small groups and prayer-partners can find ideas for collectively implementing the prayer under "Practice Together." Questions for reflection and discussion are noted in the "Consider" segment. Other resources complete the chapter in "Study Further." The basic steps of each prayer are summarized in an appendix at the end of the book for quick reference when praying.

Cultivating Prayer-Habits for the Whole Person

There are three basic kinds of prayer here: head, heart, and body. Head prayer generates from the mind and the world of ideas; it makes use of one's intellect. Heart prayer focuses outward and accesses one's social awareness. Body prayer is physically engaged, employing one's gut instincts and feelings.[4]

Each seeks to connect with a different aspect of the whole person, and each of us will find a comfort zone in one of the three. As a result, we will naturally feel more competent at that one and surer of its benefits. The other methods, the kinds that draw on our less developed qualities, will gently challenge us. To ease us into these "new" types of prayer, each of the ten practices in this book engages at least two of these comfort zones.

Circumstances and spiritual needs change over time. We may learn some of these systems now, but come to rely upon them only later. Others may be perfect for our current situations. The amount of time we can commit to prayer and the amount of energy we can give to practicing may also influence our sense of a method's usefulness. Furthermore, if we practice these methods of prayer with spiritual friends, we might attempt even the kinds of prayer that do not immediately capture our own interests because they will benefit others around us.

It is important to pray together. Not only do we descend from a spiritual lineage, we also dwell in a

---

4 Richard Rohr and Andreas Ebert, *Discovering the Enneagram: An Ancient Tool for a New Spiritual Journey* (New York: Crossroad, 1990).

contemporary community of believers. We must find likeminded people, who share our desire to know God, and join them in seeking God because that is how God has designed his family to work (Heb 10:25). We cannot know him fully without experiencing him in the company of others.

When we pray as a group, we may feel a little nervous about praying aloud or sharing specifics because prayer at its best is an intimate experience. The simple act of prayer points out our vulnerability, both to ourselves and to those who pray with us. The prospect of this vulnerability may be frightening, so hold gently what someone else reveals. The hope is that in listening to one another, we will get to know, learn from, and eventually come to trust each other. When members take the perspective that they are both humble servants and secure children of the Almighty, fears drop away and pray-ers begin to enjoy one another and to grow in their communion with God.

Communicating and Communing

Growing up in my family, we prayed "evangelical," which is to say extemporaneously and, in the case of my mother during family devotions, *really* long. Now as an adult, I realize that I often pray because it is part of my all-or-nothing personality to do so. I am either tasking at 120 percent or crashing. Prayer fits the demands of both scenarios: In my quest to listen continuously to the Holy Spirit, I often pervert prayer into a mere accomplishment on my obedience "to do" list. When I encounter the limits of my abilities to hear and obey, I turn to prayer as a last resort in the midst of my exhaustion.

What I need is something more balanced: to be still (Ps 46:10) so I can listen to God and to others, to find my center, and to be moved, not by my own frenetic physical or mental activity, but by the power of the resurrection (Phil 3:9–11). Margaret Guenther echoes Psalm 46, "We can get so tangled up in our devotional patterns—our idea of what we should be doing and how we should be praying—that we forget what we are about. We can forget the Lord's injunction to 'be still and know that I am God.' From time to time, we need to stop and savor the stillness."[5]

So I attempt to sit still with him, realizing that I can neither pray God into answering me, nor into answering me as I choose. I am obliged to acknowledge that God is Other; he transcends my understanding. What I know of him, I know because he has revealed himself to me. I want to learn to praise him as Other, rather than as an outgrowth of my needs.

Prayer, like Scripture-reading, can be a way of knowing the Other. Reading about prayer in this book may help us to pray better, but examining different approaches to prayer is not the same thing as experiencing them. In studying prayer, we need to challenge ourselves to wait and listen as disciplines of yielding to God. In practicing these methods with other people, we want to see examples of waiting and listening to God.

---

5 Margaret Guenther, *The Practice of Prayer*, vol. 4 in *The New Church's Teaching Series* (Cambridge, Mass.: Cowley, 1998), 155.

We describe prayer as *communication* with God—give and take. In prayer we entreat, praise, thank, and make confession to him. And through prayer we receive direction, encouragement, peace, conviction, rebuke, and mercy from him.

But prayer is also *communion* with God—a sense of connection and unity, belonging and being. "I am convinced that prayer is not so much something we *do* or *say* as how we *are*," writes Margaret Guenther, "grateful, questioning, penitent, comfortable, adoring, sometimes listening carefully, sometimes silently companionable. But always open and attentive."[6]

Prayer fosters relationship by improving the actual give and take with God, but it does more than that. It transforms our communication abilities into the very skills of Christ. Scripture says that the Holy Spirit intercedes with God on our behalf using "sighs too deep for words" (Rom 8:26). Access to this sort of nonverbal contact is the benefit of spending time with the invisible God. We know and speak our own minds with more clarity. We listen more attentively. We recognize God's voice and distinguish it from the many other calls in our day-to-day lives.

"But how?" many will ask. "How can I know whether or not I'm hearing God? Maybe it's just my own thoughts or maybe it's the influence of someone else. How can I be sure prayer is 'working'?"

Some of us are so sure of our own inner voices that it is pretty clear when a thought is other than our own, but we

---

[6] Ibid.

still question the nature of this other source and find it difficult to identify God's words from other strong contenders, much less trust them. Some of us may be so busy collecting information and experiences or worrying about details that we catalogue God's words without feeling the contentment of a heart-to-heart conversation. And some of us are so in tune with people around us that it is difficult to imagine "hearing" God or feeling worthy of his personal interest without the visible social cues we usually rely on.

"How can we be sure it's God talking?" The briefest, most honest answer to this important question is, "We can't. We can never be absolutely, one-hundred percent, empirically certain that God has spoken to us." But we can learn to recognize and distinguish his voice from our own, from others outside of us, and from the darkness. Just as with human relationships, the more time we spend with God, the better we know him. We are not abandoned to guessing, nor is prayer a waste of time.

It *is* possible to know when a thought or feeling is *not* God. Scripture is a reliable test of truth. For this reason, several of the following methods base prayer on portions of the Bible. We can trust that if our thoughts contradict established doctrines of Scripture, then they are not from God. Furthermore, we are not alone in our attempts to listen to the Holy Spirit. God has provided us with a community of believers whose ears are also tuned to him. Our spiritual friends can confirm or add course-corrections to our understanding of God's words to us. Finally, if we have not found peace about something, in spite of our prayers, we can continue to wait faithfully on God, trusting that he will speak in his time.

Persistence in prayer, especially during the dry times when God does not seem to be speaking, can be difficult, but if nothing else it is an act of obedience to one whom we call Lord (Deut 4:29; Jer 29:12–14). Because prayer expects perseverance, we consider it a spiritual discipline. As with all disciplines, we learn best by doing, but this can be difficult work. Prayer is deep and intimate. It might hurt to feel so exposed, and it will certainly reveal our neediness. Our human tendency is to avoid this exposure, this pain, and the change that results.

In *Exploring Spiritual Direction,* Alan Jones suggests that "one way of avoiding . . . inner revolution is, paradoxically, to become an expert."[7] Proficiency builds a wall behind which we can hide our deepest, messiest selves. Or a cage where we can jail them. Appealing to our expert-like authority may inhibit the exchange that praying was meant to foster. So, while there is no advantage to being inept and there are benefits to knowing the various methods that we can learn here, I would encourage us to push past our expertise and make ourselves available to God and to others as we pray.

Prayer is a conversation with God, a conversation we did not begin. Before a word is on our tongues, he knows it completely (Ps 139:4). Whether we realize it or not, it is always God who starts the dialogue. Thus prayer is telling

---

[7] Alan Jones, *Exploring Spiritual Direction* (new ed.; Cambridge, Mass.: Cowley, 1999), 59.

God what we want and need, but it is more. Prayer is also listening to him, and it is in the listening that we see and feel his power. In fact, if prayer does not include hearing the Holy Spirit and following his lead, then it can be pretty boring—just you repeating your agenda to God, or even more tedious, you listening to me reiterate my agenda. So before we are ready to speak God's will back to him, we must ready ourselves to hear and recognize God's will by listening. The following exercises insist on both.

Breath Prayer

Breath prayer is a short petition, repeated in the space of one inhalation-exhalation cycle, that acknowledges the natures of both the Lord and the petitioner.

BREATH PRAYER is an ancient form that arose in the fourth century among church fathers, such as Gregory of Nyssa, as a way to contemplation and as a way to "pray without ceasing" (1 Thess 5:17). Today, we are familiar with immediate breath prayers like Anne Lamott's "Help me, help me, help me. Thank you, thank you, thank you."[8] Indeed most breath prayers are short petitions that acknowledge who the Lord is and who the petitioner is.[9] They often repeat, following the rhythm of inhaling and exhaling, and the goal is to so fix them in the mind that they become as involuntary and as vital as breathing. The most famous of these is the Jesus Prayer: "Lord Jesus Christ, Son of God, have mercy on me, a sinner" (Ps 51:1; Matt 15:22; Luke 18:13).

After the Great Schism of 1054, this prayer continued in the Eastern branch of the church as a path to stillness. Not until the nineteenth century did the Jesus Prayer emerge again in the Western world. Among others, Father

---

[8] Anne Lamott, *Traveling Mercies: Some Thoughts on Faith* (New York: Anchor, 1999), 82.

[9] Richard J. Foster, *Prayer: Finding the Heart's True Home* (New York: HarperSanFrancisco, 1992), 123.

Sophrony the Archimandrite (1893–1938) brought the practice with him from Russia when he founded a monastery in Britain.[10]

Growing up in an Orthodox family, Sophrony had learned to pray for an hour at a time without tiring. However with the onset of the Russian Revolution, he rejected the Christian approach to God and sought instead an abstract Absolute through painting and yoga. He immigrated to Paris in 1921. One night as he wandered the streets, feeling spiritually void, he remembered the phrase "I am that I am" (Exod 3:14) and reawakened to the living, eternal God. His realization led him to confess that God cannot be pinned down by rational processes or by imagination. Instead the deep love within us responds to the infinite Love that is the divine. We humans are not closed containers; we are dynamic creatures, shaped by relationship with God.

Sophrony wanted to learn *how* to grow in this union with God, so he entered the monastery at Mount Athos. There he met Saint Silouan, an illiterate peasant monk. Watching the man, he could see the profound experience of God that Silouan practiced in spite of his simplicity. "If you are minded to pray in your heart and are not able," Silouan told him, "repeat the words of your prayer with your lips and keep your mind on the words you are saying. . . . In time the Lord will give you interior prayer without

---

[10] The following story and instructions are influenced by Brother Ramon and Simon Barrington-Ward, *Praying the Jesus Prayer Together* (Peabody, Mass.: Hendrickson, 2004), 39–41, 55–58, 118–29.

distraction, and you will pray with ease."[11] Sophrony became Silouan's scribe until the saint's death in 1938, and eventually moved to Essex, establishing a community that continues to reflect Silouan's habits of communion with God, including meditation through the repetition of breath prayers.

Most religions practice some form of meditation, and its physiological impact is documented by science. The difference between mantras like "om" and breath prayer is that as believers we direct prayer to the God we trust, rather than opening ourselves to an abstract other or even seeking self. We recognize the "zone" that meditation achieves because it is similar to what happens when we sit in front of the TV, or scrub a dirty floor, or play a rote video game. With the repetitious work of breath prayer, however, we discipline the frenetic upper layers of the mind to continually return to Jesus, while allowing deeper thoughts and feelings to rise to the surface, be recognized, and be yielded to him.

Sophrony reminds us that "the way to the Father lies uniquely through the Son, only-begotten and consubstantial [one] with the Father" (John 3:16; 10:30).[12] Jesus mediates our union with God because he is one with God already, and we can rest in the promise that he shares this union with us as we seek him (17:20–21). "He alone, 'knows the

---

[11] Staretz Silouan, *Wisdom from Mount Athos: The Writings of Staretz Silouan 1866–1938* (ed. Archimandrite Sophrony; trans. Rosemary Edmonds; London: Mowbrays, 1974), 83.

[12] Archimandrite Sophrony, foreword to *Wisdom from Mount Athos: The Writings of Staretz Silouan 1866–1938*, by Staretz Silouan (ed. Archimandrite Sophrony; trans. Rosemary Edmonds; London: Mowbrays, 1974), 6.

Father' with complete knowledge, and 'no man cometh unto the Father, but by the Son'" (14:6). This knowledge, Sophrony says, "is acquired through prayer of the mind united with the heart, and our whole being given over to God."[13]

When we seek communion with the Trinity using breath prayer, the prayer functions as a still place of peace. Awareness of our relationship with God grows like a bubble, expanding outward as we pass through our chaotic world. Instead of the chaos invading our spirits, breath prayer offers the protection of peace (Phil 4:7). For those of us who, like Sophrony, tend to induce self-forgetfulness through yoga, art, or—in our modern day—the internet, breath prayer helps release stress to Jesus instead of merely escaping it. It engages the body instead of placating it, so that turmoil is stilled and we are renewed for action in the world.

For those of us who are attuned to our environments, perhaps even ruled by social circumstances, breath prayer can help us stay connected to God. As a regular daily practice, the prayer keeps us humble and reminds us that we are loved, regardless of how others respond. Because it articulates who God is and who we are, it helps us maintain perspective and equips us to minister to others from a power that transcends our own (Heb 13:20–21).

Practice

1. Sit comfortably with your back straight and close your eyes.

---

[13] Ibid.

2. Pay attention to your breathing. Focus on breathing will probably exaggerate the intake and output a little. Wait until a comfortable rhythm has returned.

3. Ask Jesus to be present, to lead, to guide, and to protect. Invite him to draw you into the community of the Trinity.

4. Wait silently until you feel ready to begin praying.

5. When you are ready, pray in your breathing rhythm.
   - Inhale: Lord, Jesus Christ,
   - Pause: Son of God,
   - Exhale: have mercy on me, a sinner.

6. Use a prayer rope, touching one knot or bead for each repetition. A typical prayer rope is strung with a sequence of one large bead to every ten small ones. The small beads remind one to focus on the prayer. The large one allows for a pause. You may simply touch each of your fingers in succession. Through the first ten repetitions, you might pray aloud, considering the words of the prayer. As distractions arise, gently return your concentration to the words (see pp 108–109 for suggestions on how to deal with distractions).

7. When you reach the large bead on the prayer rope or your tenth finger, pause. With the first pause you might converse with the Lord about any sin that has risen to your mind. You might tell him about distractions.

8. Begin the next ten when you are ready, praying silently, attending to the flow of air and how it merges with the words. Perhaps on the second pause, a person or situation may come to mind for whom you wish to pray, "have mercy." Perhaps "on me" will shift to "on us." Maybe you will appropriate the significance of the words to a particular concern of your own, or the plea for mercy will become a praise for mercy obtained. Take time to share these with God.

9. As you begin the next ten repetitions, listen for the Lord speaking in your heart. Perhaps on the next rest, you will pause to let his words flow.

10. As the prayer repetitions begin to move from your head to your heart, you may feel a desire to still even the echo of the words and to sit quietly with the Lord in peace. When you are ready, you may begin the prayer again or move on to other disciplines of the day.

11. When the silence is gathered and before you move on to the day's tasks, write down anything that particularly stood out to you during your meditation. It may be that the prayer returns to you throughout the day with this nuance. The next time you practice the breath prayer, perhaps this will function as a starting point in your move to stillness.

12. Exercises other than breathing may also provide a physical rhythm that can fuse with the repetition of the prayer. You may wish to try an uninterrupted walk or

bicycle ride in a quiet place, reciting each phrase of your prayer with every step or pedal-pump that you take.

13. Other short petitions in Scripture or some personal breath prayer may be used instead of the Jesus Prayer, for example "Help us, O Lord our God, for we rely on you" (2 Chr 14:1) or "Lamb of God, who takes away the sin of the world, have mercy on me" (John 1:29). As you regularly practice breath prayer, it will eventually enter into other daily activities like a song you cannot get out of your head. If the repetition becomes annoying or void of meaning, return with intention to the words, retaking them as a prayer for the moment.

Sample the Prayer

It is possible to incorporate breath prayer into one's daily routine, even if uninterrupted times for meditation are not available. It is doubtful that the Canaanite woman, who spoke one of the first variations of the Jesus Prayer (Matt 15:22), had the leisure to sit still either. Like her, we can turn to Jesus throughout the day as needs arise, weaving one or two repetitions of the prayer into the fabric of that incident, sometimes without even pausing our current activity.

Practice Together

Many of us are already accustomed to repeating prayers together. For example, we may say the Lord's Prayer in unison every Sunday during worship. Breath prayer takes a little more work, since we all breathe at different rates and meditation can be difficult or awkward if we cannot let go of our awareness of those around us. However, practicing this prayer together offers several benefits. Hearing others calm their breathing and center down may coach us to do the same without having to concentrate so hard. Also, listening to the Holy Spirit as he speaks to and through others around us may help us tune our ears to what he would say to our own hearts.

Choose a breath prayer that appeals to the characteristics or circumstances of your particular group. Say the words of the prayer together a couple of times, just to practice the sounds and the pauses. Designate one person to lead the prayer and make yourselves comfortable around the room. Take a few moments to "listen" to the silence while you calm your breathing. The leader can begin by inviting Jesus to draw you together into the communion of the Trinity and to guide and protect you as you seek him in the stillness.

When all seem ready, pray the first ten rounds out loud together and pause. The leader can then invite people to mention to the Lord any distractions or bits of trivia that have risen to mind during the repetitions. It can be amusing to hear the free associations that others' minds make. Allow the laughter and when it dies down, wait in silence.

Pray the second ten rounds out loud together and pause. Invite participants to pray sentence prayers of confession concerning any sin that the Lord may have brought to mind. Again, wait in silence.

For the third ten, let the leader pray aloud, while members pray in their breathing rhythms. At the pause, the leader can invite participants to pray the Lord's mercy on specific people or for specific situations, including themselves. Then keep silence together, listening for him to speak.

During the fourth round of ten, the leader and members can pray silently in their breathing rhythms, allowing the Lord to say what he will. When sufficient silence has been kept, the leader can thank the Lord for his presence and close the season of prayer.

Come back to the circle and share what God has brought to mind as you centered on him. What, if anything, stood out to you in the practice of this prayer? If you simply feel blank, what is the nothing like? As you discuss your individual experiences, do any themes or directions for the group arise? What might the Lord be saying to your community? What further response might you consider?

As your group becomes more comfortable praying this way together, you may wish to apply less structure to the repetitions. As you still yourselves for prayer, one person may begin the prayer, establishing the rhythm, and continuing through fifty repetitions. Others may join in verbally and drop out to pray in their breathing rhythm along the way. After the first fifty, another person may take over the lead, maintaining the oral rhythm while some join in aloud and others drop out.[14]

---

[14] Brother Ramon, *A Hidden Fire: Exploring the Deeper Reaches of Prayer* (Hants, England: Marshall Pickering, 1987), 118.

Consider

1. The Jesus Prayer arises from several passages in Scripture. Look up Matthew 15:22 and Mark 10:47. What is the significance of the title "son of David"? Why do you think church tradition transformed this into "son of God"? See also Luke 18:13.

2. What is the significance of the phrase, "I am that I am" (Exod 3:14)? Why do you suppose it affected Sophrony the way it did?

3. How would your friends praying in unison with you be different than praying alone? What would be the advantage of another person praying aloud while you prayed silently?

4. If you were to compose your own breath prayer, what would it be about? Think for a moment. Which of God's names would you choose to acknowledge who the Lord is? What words would you use to characterize yourself? What would be your petition? How could you shorten it so that it could truly follow the rhythm of your breath?

Study Further

Blythe, Theresa A. Pages 38–40, 86–87, 158–159, and 181 in 50 Ways to Pray: Practices from Many Traditions and Times. Nashville, Tenn.: Abingdon, 2006.

Brother Ramon. A Hidden Fire: Exploring the Deeper Reaches of Prayer. Hants, England: Marshall Pickering, 1987.

Brother Ramon and Simon Barrington-Ward. Praying the Jesus Prayer Together. Peabody, Mass.: Hendrickson, 2004.

Foster, Richard J. "Unceasing Prayer." Pages 122–24 in Prayer: Finding the Heart's True Home. New York: HarperSanFrancisco, 1992.

Guenther, Margaret. "The Jesus Prayer." Pages 69–72 in The Practice of Prayer. Volume 4 in The New Church's Teaching Series. Cambridge, Mass.: Cowley, 1998.

Mayfield, Sue. Pages 25–26 in Exploring Prayer. Peabody, Mass.: Hendrickson, 2007.

Staretz Silouan. Wisdom from Mount Athos: The Writings of Staretz Silouan 1866–1938. Edited by Archimandrite Sophrony. Translated by Rosemary Edmonds. London: Mowbrays, 1974.

Thurston, Bonnie. "Praying the Name: The Jesus Prayer." Pages 86–104 in For God Alone: A Primer on Prayer. Notre Dame, Ind.: University of Notre Dame Press, 2009.

Wolpert, Daniel. "The Jesus Prayer: There Is Power in His Name." Pages 51–62 and 177–78 in Creating a Life with God: The Call of Ancient Prayer Practices. Nashville, Tenn.: Upper Room, 2003.

Music Prayer

BARTH'S BALANCE OF DOGMA AND PLAY

Music prayer employs lyrics and notes in a unified expression of both the principles and the playfulness of our relationships with God.

MUSIC PRAYER often expresses our cries and our praises to the Lord better than verbal prayer alone (Ps 55:1; 92:1). In music prayer the right-brain's creativity combines with the left-brain's sense of pattern. Literal meaning in the lyrics melds with emotional meaning in the harmonies. When we respond by singing along or clapping to the rhythm, prayer rises from voice and movement, as well as from reason. And when we are hearing with this fuller understanding, music prayer broadens our minds to the possibilities of God's response (Ps 81:1–10).

However, even church music is not prayer unless we offer it to God or receive it as though it is from him (Amos 6:4–6). We have all listened to Christmas carols, for example, as a seasonal backdrop, without noticing the person to whom they refer. On the other hand, music that is not strictly sacred can also stretch us beyond ourselves and cause us to reach for the "Other" that is God (Exod 15:11; Isa 55:8–9). This, too, can be considered prayer.

Both the sacred and secular music of Mozart provided just such a vehicle for multifaceted prayer throughout the work of theologian Karl Barth (1886–1968), a man whose life was engrossed with systems for articulating truth and establishing moral order.

Born in Switzerland to a theological lecturer at the university of Basel, Barth spent his own early academic career in Germany. He studied under the powerful liberal Protestant minds of the nineteenth century, but his theology began to change in 1911 when he entered the pastorate of a small Reformed church just over the border in Switzerland.

From that politically neutral vantage, he and his congregation listened in horror as the guns of World War I demolished countless lives and with them, nineteenth century idealism. To Barth's further dismay, many of his former professors endorsed Kaiser Wilhelm's war, claiming that God's will was being worked out in the emperor's war policy[15] (Isa 5:20).

Discouraged by the flimsy beliefs he had learned from these teachers, Barth began to search for a more robust system of understanding the institutional and individual sins that war had uncovered (Rom 3:21–23). He found the popular Protestant theology of Germany, where he was now teaching, too optimistic concerning humanity. It squared neither with the ugly reality of world war, nor with Scripture. Freedom from evil, Barth said, could not be attained in the human experience of truth, but only in God's self-disclosure (2 Cor 3:17–18).

In his prolific writings, Barth insisted that human pride corrupted even organized and personal religion, all of which fell under God's judgment (Rom 2:6–9). The 1930s

---

[15] Millard J. Erickson, *Christian Theology* (one-vol. ed.; Grand Rapids, Mich.: Baker, 1985), 163.

confirmed his worst suspicions when a large segment of Germany's state church threw its support behind the Nazi movement. Millions of Jews were murdered while the church claimed that God's will was being revealed through Hitler's plans. Barth's objections drove him out of Germany and back to Basel, where he continued to write.

Eventually, his writings would radically reform Protestant theology. His multivolume *Church Dogmatics* continues to be the most comprehensive systematic theology since the war. However for Barth, this ardent advocacy of right thinking was more than an academic endeavor. In Barth's mind, sound doctrine actually changed a person. "To know God, to have correct information about him, [was] to be related to him in a salvific experience."[16]

On the other hand, Barth understood that communing with God was not limited by how perfectly he could conceptualize God (Rom 11:33). To balance his focus on objective moral principles, Barth immersed himself in the music of Mozart though he confessed, "I haven't the vaguest idea of the theory of harmony or of the mysteries of counterpoint."[17] Nevertheless, "I have for years and years begun each day with Mozart, and only then . . . turned to my *Dogmatics*. . . . How am I to explain this? In a few

---

16 Ibid., 163.

17 Karl Barth, "A Letter of Thanks to Mozart," *Luzerner Neuesten Nachrichten* (21 January 1956) repr. in *Wolfgang Amadeus Mozart* (trans. Clarence K. Pott; Grand Rapids, Mich.: Eerdmans, 1986), 20.

words perhaps this way: our daily bread must also include playing."[18]

Unlike Barth, Mozart revealed no doctrine in his music.[19] Barth wrote, "[he] does not demand that [the listener] make any decisions or take any positions; he simply leaves him free."[20] Barth understood Mozart's music to independently complement the "objective statements of the sacred texts . . . often in a very surprising way."[21]

Barth could receive Mozart in all his playfulness; he could even play along, because Mozart gave voice to "real life in all its discord."[22] Freedom could be experienced in Mozart's music because Mozart disciplined himself not to play to the extremes, but called the listener "to see himself as the person he really [was]"[23] (John 8:31–36). "What then came forth was always, and still is, an invitation to the listener to venture, just a little out of the snail's shell of his own subjectivity."[24]

In the midst of Barth's struggle to reintroduce the Continent's churches to unchangeable truth, he found

[18] Karl Barth, "A Testimonial to Mozart," *Neue Zürcher Zeitung* (13 February 1955); repr. in *Wolfgang Amadeus Mozart* (trans. Clarence K. Pott; Grand Rapids, Mich.: Eerdmans, 1986), 16.
[19] Karl Barth, "Mozart's Freedom" (an address delivered at the Commemorative Celebration in the Music Hall in Basel, 29 January 1956) repr. in *Wolfgang Amadeus Mozart* (trans. Clarence K. Pott; Grand Rapids, Mich.: Eerdmans, 1986), 53.
[20] Karl Barth, "Wolfgang Amadeus Mozart," *Zwingli-Kalender* (Basel: Friedrich Reinhardt, 1956); repr. in *Wolfgang Amadeus Mozart* (trans. Clarence K. Pott; Grand Rapids, Mich.: Eerdmans, 1986), 37.
[21] Ibid., 39.
[22] Ibid., 33.
[23] Barth, "Mozart's Freedom," 54–55.
[24] Ibid., 50.

himself moved to prayer by the very subjective tug of Mozart's music. "Does not every *Kyrie*," he wrote, "every *Miserere,* no matter how darkly foreboding its beginning, sound as if borne upward by the trust that the plea for mercy was granted long ago? . . . In Mozart's version . . . *Dona nobis pacem!* [*Grant us peace!*] is a prayer, but a prayer already answered"[25] (Ps 51:1; John 14:27).

Barth's instinct toward balancing cognitive and emotional understanding was not unfounded. Composing in the eighteenth century for the Catholic church, Mozart himself had challenged Protestantism that it was too much "in the head."[26]

Listening to music filled out Barth's work toward a durable set of doctrines. The music renewed a childlike *delight* in God's grace, and delight brought deep joy to the process of accurately *describing* God's grace. Music aired the longing of his heart in a way that systematics could not.

It can do the same for us. If, like Barth, we are motivated by good behavior and accurate systems that undergird our ideals, we can be tempted to allow the struggle against imperfection to become our only means of interacting with God (Eph 2:8–9). Through music prayer, we learn to play with God, not just study him. Music gives our ideals voice and hope, lifting our heads out of the fight for perfection and reminding us to delight in the process of getting to know God and being known by him (Ps 37:1–4).

---

[25] Ibid., 56.
[26] Barth, "Wolfgang Amadeus Mozart," 26.

If on the other hand, we tend too much toward play, planning the next experience, or partying to drown out hurt, praying through music can ground our gifts of happiness in principles of Scripture (Eph 5:18–20). Music can fill us with the durable joy we find in hearing God's song and singing it back to him. In music, we are able to maintain our childlike outlook, while discovering a deep delight that sustains us in the midst of pain as well as pleasure (Ps 5:11; 131:1–2).

Practice

1. Think about the kind of music that stirs you. Consider your church's style of worship, the tunes you listen to in the car, and music you own or request for gifts. Does this music provide a vehicle for prayer already? Perhaps you will wish to do a little research to find a style of sacred music that is more in keeping with your preferences than whatever your church uses. Or you might want to break out of your listening habits and try something different. In any case, find a piece of music that moves you.

2. Consider the lyrics. If you cannot understand the language, find a translation. Often classical church music is sung in Latin, but the program or liner notes include a translation for English-speakers. If not, you may be able to type the title of the piece into your search engine to find a translation online. Alternatively, you may find that translating the words yourself provides the interaction you need to truly consider the meaning. Even if they are in English, read them from   the liner anyway, or write them

down as you hear them. What is the composer saying? What is the context of the song? What do the words mean to you? What aspect of your own life do they touch upon? If the music is not sacred music, how do the words nevertheless express your thoughts to God?

3. Pray the words aloud (in English) without the music, listening to the meaning they evoke. Do they praise God's character, offer him thanks, beseech his presence or his promises, make confession? How is it that they speak for you at this time?

4. Listen to the music again. Hear the words, whether in English or not. Notice how your heart rate and breathing respond as you anticipate the music. Feel the meaning of the words working through the music.

5. Now close your eyes and listen to the piece. Resist the urge to understand or pick out specific words, instruments, or rhythms. Hear the whole music.

6. Listen a third time, allowing the piece and your response to speak to God on behalf of yourself and others. What are you saying to him? What might he be saying to you?

7. The previous steps begin with an analytical approach and move into hearing the whole music and allowing it to become prayer. Over time this process may grow less intentional, more organic. If you find the playfulness of your music time with God turning into background noise

again, return to the piece-by-piece process and retake the music as your song to God.

8. Make a written note of how the music, the words, and your own petitions intersected as you prayed. Or share this with your small group or a spiritual friend.

Sample the Prayer

If your time is limited, take a significant piece of music with you throughout your day and repeat it at appropriate intervals, on the train or in your car as you commute, on your headset as you walk the dog or take your daily exercise, piped throughout the house as you dust. With each repetition, practice one of the listening steps (4–6) above. Choose another piece for the next day. Each day, notice how or when the lyrics and music return to you and speak for you or the circumstances in the non-listening portions of your day. What are you saying to God about the situation? What might he be saying to you?

Practice Together

Consider sharing your personal pieces of music prayer with your group. Members can take turns explaining how their music expresses their communion with God. Then as the group listens, they can play a recording of the piece or an excerpt so that the full impact can be felt by all.

Think about using music for a group prayer. Perhaps a musician in the group can lead everyone on a guitar or piano or perhaps a recording can be played. Consider the lyrics and the music separately and then together as above.

If it is appropriate, the group may want to sing the piece together. After this time of meditation, share with one another how the words, the music, and your own petitions for the group intersected.

Consider

1. Why do you suppose Mozart thought Protestant prayer was "all in the head"? What differences in the prayer emphases of Protestant, Roman Catholic, and Orthodox traditions have you noticed?

2. Have you ever suffered life-altering disappointment? For Barth, the two world wars changed not only the way he thought about God, but the way he interacted with him. What impact did your experience have on your ability, desire, or understanding of prayer? If music played a role, how did it influence your conversations with God?

3. How does the nature of your prayer change as you become more and more familiar with the music and the lyrics? What are the advantages of familiarity in this kind of prayer? How do new pieces of music benefit your communion with God?

4. What is the impact of singing along with recorded or live music? Do you find it more or less difficult to pray with music if you hear it performed live? Why do you think this is? Have you ever performed music either as part of a worship service or in a concert? How does this influence the intimacy of the music as your prayer?

5. How does listening with another person or as a group modify the dynamic of prayer in music? How do watching and listening to other people's "interpretations" of the piece help or hinder you in offering the music to God? Hearing from him?

Study Further

Barth, Karl. *Wolfgang Amadeus Mozart.* Translated by Clarence K. Pott. Grand Rapids, Mich., Eerdmans, 1986.

Blythe, Theresa A. "Lectio Divina with Music." Pages 52–55 and 165–66 in *50 Ways to Pray: Practices from Many Traditions and Times.* Nashville, Tenn.: Abingdon, 2006.

Foster, Richard J. Pages 110–11, 135–36 in *Prayer: Finding the Heart's True Home.* New York: HarperSan-Francisco, 1992.

Mayfield, Sue. "Praying with Music. Pages 87–91 in *Exploring Prayer.* Peabody, Mass.: Hendrickson, 2007.

Action Prayer
THÉRÈSE'S LITTLE WAY IN THE MIDST OF THE
MUNDANE

Action prayer is nonverbal communication to God, using our attitudes and our attempts to obey, which draws its energy from Christ's example and empowerment.

WE ARE ACCUSTOMED to thinking of prayer as verbal—an exchange of words—or at least mental, a centering-down of thoughts that allows stillness to grow in us as we make our way through the daily mill. With the Little Way, we intentionally press further, drawing the outer world inward as we intersect with it and respond to it. Our actions and reactions become the prayer. We are transformed into givers as we practice giving, into listeners because we listen, into champions as we defend the weak, into the image of Christ because we act like Christ (Col 3:10). Our lives themselves address God directly. Thérèse Martin,[27] a French nun, sought to practice this sort of embodied prayer.

Thérèse (1873–1897) was the youngest of nine. Her mother died when she was four years old, and the loss plunged her into a childhood of insecurity. When she was thirteen, however, she found in Jesus' birth the comfort of one who understood her vulnerability. At a Christmas Eve service, she tells that "the sweet infant Jesus, scarce yet an

---

27 The following story of Thérèse Martin's life relies on Thomas Plassmann, *Lives of Saints with Excerpts from Their Writings* (New York: Crawley, 1954), n.p. [cited 12 Jan 2006]. Online: www.ewtn.com/therese/therese1.htm.

hour old, flooded with his glorious sunshine the darkness into which my soul was plunged. In becoming weak and little for love of me, he made me strong and brave."[28] She never lost her sensitivity, but in Jesus she also found a child-like humility with which to engage the world.

At the age of fifteen, she sought to join the Carmelite religious order in Lisieux, a small town in Normandy. Initially the superior declined her application because of her age, but the girl's steady character eventually won out. She made her final vows two years later and was soon raised to assist the mistress of novices. Her abbess assigned her the job of writing an autobiography when she was twenty-two, and we have this work as *The Story of a Soul*.[29] A year later, after her death from tuberculosis, the history circulated among the convents and eventually acquired a large following.

Declaring spiritual disciplines, even the rosary, too involved for her, Thérèse practiced what she called the Little Way. She read the Bible, and her verbal prayers were direct and personal—an unpretentious toddler telling her father what she wanted and trusting him to provide. Trivial actions done for God's glory became her nonverbal prayer. Life, she said, presented sufficient challenges and opportunities for grace without complicating the matter. Instead of adding special spiritual disciplines, she sought to do ordinary things with extraordinary love. "The smallest

---

[28] Thérèse of Lisieux, *Saint Thérèse of Lisieux: An Autobiography* (trans. Thomas N. Taylor; London: Burns, Oates, & Washbourne, 1927), 86.
[29] Thérèse of Lisieux, *The Story of a Soul* (trans. John Beevers; New York: Image, 1989).

action, done with love, [was] more important than great deeds done for personal glory, gratification, or simply out of obedience."[30]

As an example of her plan, Thérèse noted an instance that occurred one day during meditation. As the sisters waited in quiet contemplation, one of them fidgeted incessantly with her rosary beads until Thérèse felt crazed with irritation. She wanted to turn and glare the nun into silence. She became so frustrated that she began to sweat. At last, she writes, "instead of vainly attempting not to hear it, I set myself to listen attentively as though it were delightful music, and my meditation—which was not the prayer of 'quiet'—was passed in offering this music to Our Lord."[31]

In Thérèse's Little Way, we too can find an open path to engagement with Jesus, even when verbal prayer is drowned out. We are accustomed to thinking of prayer as solely conversation, an exchange of words. God does make himself known through language (John 1:1); however, our relationship with him is not "just talk." Though we could not know God if he did not speak to us through Scriptures and by his Son, God also reveals himself in nature and in his actions (Rom 1:19–20; Ps 98:2; Jer 33:6). In the same way, we reveal and yield our wills to God by our actions, as well as our speech (Jas 1:22–25).

As we respond to others, Jesus is the one who receives our replies (Mic 6:6–8). When we act instead of avoiding

---

[30] Society of the Little Flower, "Learn about Therese," n.p. [cited 20 June 2008]. Online: www.littleflower.org/learn/faq.asp.

[31] Thérèse, *Autobiography*, 186.

the work or the person, he is the one we obey. Even as we wait for the right service-projects, skills-fit, or timing, this formation prayer takes advantage of the incidents and interpersonal encounters that occur daily. We begin to see everyday actions and reactions as our communion with him. By allowing what we do to contribute to our conversation with God, we permit him to transform us in the areas of action and emotion, not just thought.

For those of us whose defaults already tend toward help and service, practicing the Little Way transforms both our acknowledged and our unknown motives into intentional choices for Jesus. Even when we fear that our kindnesses will not be reciprocated, we choose to trust our Father to enfold us and Jesus to satisfy our needs for belonging and welcome. Then we can participate without needing affirmation from our fellows because God himself receives and delights in our service. We look to please God, instead of depending on others to notice and respond to our giving (Matt 6:1–6). Without expectation of reward or thanks to refuel us, we act from Jesus' strength and with his bravery. And in acting *from* his character, we are changed *into* his character.

Practice

1. As you pass through your day, yield to God the tasks that you do and the reactions that you feel.

2. Give him your irritation, your delight, or whatever emotion you feel because that is what you have to give. Offer him both your desire to respond unselfishly and your

actual response. Do not waste energy pretending or attempting on your own to *feel* the way you "should." Instead, ask Christ to receive your disgruntled feelings and to reshape them into something that you are pleased to give and that God is pleased to receive. Offer your attitude honestly. Then *act* as Jesus has asked. With the incarnation, Jesus became weak, so that you could act from his strength. Offer your actions to God as your prayer.

3. If you mop vigorously, then let the vigor be your prayer and the mop be your tongue. Some actions allow our minds to multitask and it may be possible to think prayer words as well, but do not lose the language of action just because words are available. If you play the piano tentatively, then offer God the tentative music that you are able to make. Are you on the phone with clients all day? Then let the nature of your cooperation in work be your worship. If you are asked to photocopy, even when it is not really your job, then pray by your submission to God and your excellence in photocopying.

4. There is a difference between practicing the Little Way and enabling an abuser. If you are not safe because of another's actions or verbal attacks, it is right to remove yourself from the situation and seek help. The Little Way is a practice for the countless other times in the daily grind when accommodating the people around you would honor God as a yielded response to him.

5. The goal of this method of prayer is to conquer your

...ide in order to foster communion with Jesus, so it may take some practice. When you forget or fail, remember that you are only a toddler. Allow the Father to pick you up and comfort you. Know that Jesus, too, made himself vulnerable, and it is his brotherhood that enables you to follow in this Little Way. Consider his pleasure in your attempts to be like him. Hear his word of encouragement and appreciation. God does not "need" your success, but his heart swells with joy at your desire to be with him and to share in his work.

6. At the end of the day, record what you learned or received as you exercised this nonverbal communication with Jesus. How did he sustain you in the practice?

7. Return to the Scripture and perhaps to verbal prayer. Ask the Lord to feed your spirit with his Word.

Sample the Prayer

If committing a whole day to this sort of embodied prayer seems like a deterrent to ever getting started, consider designating 15 or 30 minutes to it. For example, if your workday begins at 9:00 a.m., give yourself a chance to get settled and then practice this prayer of action from 9:30 to 9:45. Use this timeframe every day for a week and then pick another 15-minute slot. Begin with a period that is likely to include few people. Move to one with more interaction or expand your timeframe as you grow confident in the practice.

Practice Together

There is something about teamwork that can be sweet to watch and exciting to participate in. When every member contributes to his full potential and each contribution benefits a goal in which all believe, when people pitch in and help as others are in need and no one holds back, a group can work like a well-oiled machine. Even the interaction, not to mention the achievement of a goal, provides a thrill. Such clockwork from humans is rare, often only experienced during emergencies, but the results are deeply satisfying to the participants and uplifting to onlookers.

In the same way, small groups who defer to one another in service to others often find that they are lifted outside of themselves as individuals. Members discover the character of Christ in ways they could not have found alone. And outsiders, watching their work, are moved as much or more by the nature of the group's service as by the service itself.

Consider using this prayerful approach to govern your church committee, your volunteer work, or your ministry.

Or think about adding a service component to your small group or to your spiritual friendships. Once a month, instead of meeting for prayer, study, or fun, meet to cook for a soup kitchen, tutor children in a local school, repair or clean the home of someone in need, or some other project. Determine ahead of time that as you grow more accustomed to one another's quirks and weaknesses, you will yield to one another with intention instead of merely giving in to satisfy social norms about avoiding confrontation. As you work, allow your humility to be that of Christ (Phil 2:5–8).

After each service session, take a few moments to debrief, to discuss your difficulties, your attitudes, and your victories. Seek help from one another instead of harboring resentments and hurts (Lev 19:18; Eph 4:31). Be reconciled to one another quickly when you do fail to treat each other with humility and dignity (Matt 5:23–24). And before you leave, return your work and the nature of your work to God. With child-like faith remind yourselves that he receives your attempts to serve others as service to him and he rejoices over you (Isa 62:5).

Consider

1. What Scriptures can you think of that encourage this plan of "action as acceptable prayer"? Look at Micah 6:6–8, Matthew 6:1–6, 1 Corinthians 10:31, Colossians 3:17, and James 2:26 if you want a refresher. There are plenty of others. How do these verses nuance the way you think of embodying prayer in action.

2. Protestants of certain traditions may feel that action prayer is a recapitulation of an overly familiar "Protestant work ethic." What characteristics do action prayer and this work ethic share? How are they different? In what ways can action prayer be practiced so that the burden pray-ers feel is the "easy yoke" of Jesus' promise (Matt 11:30)?

3. Imagine or recall a disturbing incident or person you have encountered. Now think of Jesus as that person or

disruption, and move your mind through the situation with him instead of the original actor. Do not attempt to picture Jesus as mean or hurtful. He is not. Simply see him in place of that person, his image within that person (Gen 1:26). What difficulties does such a swap pose for you? What advantage might there be to modifying your behavior or your actions as if Jesus were actually the recipient?

4. Consider the communication a visual artist attempts to achieve. By depicting the world in a particular way, the painter or sculptor makes his perspective known without using words. How is this nonverbal message like the exchange of words? How is it different? How does the analogy of communicating through art expand the way you understand communicating through humble action?

5. Think about the proverb "actions speak louder than words." What do your actions reveal about you? What do they say to God? What do they say about God to those watching you?

Study Further

For the story of Thérèse Martin's life, see www.ewtn. com/therese/therese1.htm.

Foster, Richard J. "The Little Way." Pages 62–63 in *Prayer: Finding the Heart's True Home*. New York: Harper-SanFrancisco, 1992.

Hutchinson, Gloria. "Therese of Lisieux: The Woman Warrior." Pages 84–103 in *Six Ways to Pray from Six Great Saints*. Cincinnati, Ohio: St. Anthony Messenger, 1982.

Nelson, John. *Living the Little Way of Love: With Therese of Lisieux*. New York: New City, 2000.

Thérèse of Lisieux. *The Story of a Soul*. Translated by John Beevers. New York: Image, 1989.

Presence Prayer

BROTHER LAWRENCE'S SANCTUARY ON THE SPOT

Presence prayer is choosing to believe in and concentrate on God's continual attention towards us in order to increase our awareness of and dependence upon his very personal presence.

THE PURPOSE of presence prayer is both to position ourselves toward God and to become aware of his voice calling to us throughout the day, so that we increasingly note a "sense of cooperation with God in little things."[32] Like all prayer, this exercise is often characterized by seasons of deep discovery and diligent discipline. For Nicholas Herman the practice took ten years to translate from intentional choice to spontaneous habit, but the work satisfied him more than any other spiritual endeavor.

Nicholas Herman was born to a poor family of Lorraine, France, in 1611. He received no formal education and served first as a soldier and then as a household servant. In 1666, he joined a Carmelite order in Paris as a lay brother and remained there until he died in 1691. We know him as Brother Lawrence.

The one thing Brother Lawrence wanted more than anything else was to "belong entirely to God"[33] (1 Thess 5:23). He writes that throughout his service, he learned

---

[32] Frank C. Laubach, *Letters by a Modern Mystic* (Westwood, N.J.: Revell, 1937; repr. 1958), 14.
[33] Brother Lawrence, *The Practice of the Presence of God* (rev. ed.; ed. Hal M. Helms; trans. Robert J. Edmonson; Orleans, Mass.: Paraclete, 1985), 109.

many different spiritual practices for "going to God," but found these confusing. Instead, he attempted to experience the presence of God in the midst of the mundane chores of daily life. Each day he would fix the thought of Christ in his mind before he rose, and he would pray as his last act before he fell asleep. Throughout the day, he sought to return continuously to Christ, so that everything he did was guided by and given to the Spirit.

For ten years he battled straying thoughts, trying to shift the habit from a repetitive discipline of inviting Christ's presence to an involuntary act of the heart. In his letters, he describes wrestling against a wandering mind, trying not to dwell on his lapses or become discouraged. In one letter, he explained, "When I no longer thought that I would do anything other than finish my days in these troubles and anxieties, . . . I found myself suddenly changed, and my soul, which until then had always been troubled, felt a sense of deep inner peace."[34]

Brother Lawrence remained a kitchen servant all his life, referring to himself as the "lord of all pots and pans,"[35] but in his mind, no task was too trivial for God's company. This custom of minute-by-minute prayer is encapsulated in his famous quote: "The time of business does not with me differ from the time of prayer; and in the noise and clatter of my kitchen, while several persons are at the same time calling for different things, I possess God in as great

---

[34] Ibid., 110, 93.
[35] Richard J. Foster, *Prayer: Finding the Heart's True Home* (New York: HarperSanFrancisco, 1992), 124.

tranquility as if I were upon my knees at the blessed sacrament"[36] (Ps 139:7).

Some of us are drawn instinctively to the tranquility that a life of thought implies, soaking in every possible "way to God" like sponges. We crave the contemplative lifestyle of Brother Lawrence's monastery, but like him we may not have the luxury of permanent retreat. We, too, must engage daily in some sort of business. We, too, must cope with noise and clatter. Practicing God's presence grants us sanctuary in whatever situation we find ourselves. Instead of storing up methods for getting to God, we are able to get God himself and to pass his peace along to others.

This sense of sanctuary also benefits those of us who are immediate, action-oriented responders (Ps 27:4). In Brother Lawrence's exercise, our perspectives are stretched. We learn to retreat from "living large" under our own power, so we can reinvest in living within the fullness of God (John 10:10). Rather than being driven by instinct, our deeds are born in the vulnerability of abiding with the Spirit. We act with steady intention, instead of simply reacting to the challenges around us. And when we receive God's mercy through submission to him, we are able to grant his mercy to others (Matt 10:8).

In his letters, Brother Lawrence expressed reticence about instructing others in his practice. Thankfully one of the followers of this path, Frank Laubach (1884–1970), left

---

36 Brother Lawrence, *The Practice of the Presence of God* (Old Tappan, N.J.: Revell, 1958), 9.

diary entries that break down some steps to begin this lifelong discipline of awareness. Laubach, a missionary to the Philippines, notes that on the face of it, this experiment in prayer may strike one as too intense, too internally focused, or too impossible to coordinate with the myriad tasks and conversations that must be accomplished in a day.[37] "Do not try it," he warns, "unless you feel dissatisfied with your own relationship with God."[38]

Practice

1. First resolve just to start and finish each day as Brother Lawrence did, by inviting the Lord to rule your day as you think about it before you rise and by offering him the results at the end of the day before you fall asleep. Do not wait until you have mastered this habit, but set yourself a goal of several days or weeks during which you will simply invoke the Lord's presence, asking him to speak, before waking fully and before sleeping fully.

2. When you reach your mark, note any ways in which your awareness, your daily life, or anything else has changed. You may consider more practice of the same or may feel it is time to move further into the discipline.

3. Choose something regular in your day that you will use as a prompt. Perhaps it will be the sight of your favorite color, the quarter hour chime of a clock, or a daily chore such as

---

[37] Laubach, *Letters*, 11, 19.
[38] Ibid., 12.

walking the dog. Whenever your prompt appears (or sounds), pause to invite the Lord into your actions, your words, your thoughts, your emotions. Every few weeks, you may need to change your prompt to stir the practice, so that you do not become mired in habituation and miss the Lord. Think of these pauses as checking out to rest for a moment in the "chapel of your heart."[39] Perhaps you will imagine Jesus with you in your sanctuary.

4. Regularly note the impact that these rest-stops have in your ordinary life. How is the Lord present? Do you feel like you are cooperating with God in the little things? Have you begun to miss God if you wait too long to take a break with him? Do you find the practice arduous? Have other conversations or tasks changed as you seek God regularly?[40] Discuss these with a friend in the journey. Perhaps you will journal once a week so that you may revisit your notes in times of discouragement.

5. You may wish to play the game of minutes,[41] where you try to see how many minutes in a day you can be aware of God's presence.

6. Perhaps you will pick one hour each day to continuously cooperate with God, even in the littlest tasks. Ask him what

[39] Brother Lawrence, *The Practice of the Presence of God* (New York: Doubleday/Image, 1977), 65.

[40] Ibid., 29.

[41] Richard Foster, *Prayer: Finding the Heart's True Home* (New York: HarperSanFancisco, 1992), 126.

he thinks while making each decision, tightening every bolt, reading every paragraph, etc. Enjoy the perfection of that hour with him. Initially, such a goal might seem unrealistic. Laubach laments, "If one thinks of God all the time, he will never get anything else done." But he reminds himself (and us) that "concentration is merely the continuous return to the same problem from a million angles. We do not think of one thing. We always think of the relationship of at least two things, and more often of three or more things simultaneously. So my problem is this: Can I bring God back in my mind-flow every few seconds so that God shall always be in my mind as an after image, shall always be one of the elements in every concept and precept?"[42]

7. Eventually you may invite the Lord into everything, all day long, no matter how trivial, from riding the subway in a rush-hour crowd to answering customers' calls on the phone. This may be the most difficult step in concentrating on the Lord because other people's conversations and expressions distract you from your goal of hearing God. If this is the case, pray inwardly for the people you encounter, not an elaborate supplication, but a small shift of awareness, whatever reasonably allows you to remain present to that person and the business at hand. It will become easier as you turn the practice into a habit and feel a new depth and richness within the people around you.[43] Finally, consider receiving interruptions to your plans as

---

42 Laubach, *Letters*, 19–20.
43 Ibid., 58–59.

God's plan instead. See them as God's indicator to stop and listen to him.[44]

8. This exercise is called "practicing the presence of God" for a reason. It takes practice. Laubach began in a lonesome time of life and in the quiet times of the day and expanded to include interactions with people. He started by checking out of activity and in with God and then grew the exercise into a continuous habit. Talking about God with others, rather than only thinking about him, helped him stay on track. Initially, he sought God in one particular room of the house and eventually discovered that he longed to be in that room and got his best work done there because he associated it with God. When he practiced God's presence, he addressed God in the second person ("you") instead of concentrating on the abstract concept of deity. He tried to feel as though God was "just behind everything . . . just under my hand, just under the typewriter, just behind this desk, just inside the file, just inside the camera."[45] He even allowed God to talk back in his "inner life" by loosening control over his own tongue or fingers on the keyboard and noticing how the ensuing ramble or poetry spoke to him.[46]

9. Laubach noted that he hardly ever felt as though he had succeeded in being with God for a whole day. On the other hand, he asked, "Does the effort help?" And answered, "Tremendously. Nothing I have ever found proves such a

---

[44] Ibid., 61–62.

[45] Ibid., 44.

[46] Ibid., 35.

tonic to the mind and body." He acknowledged that forcing the experiment to the point of strain provided no success or relief.[47] Instead, he realized that he could let go of his perceived failures and begin again with a clean slate at any instant (Phil 3:13–14). The possibility of a fresh start encouraged him to keep going. There may be times when you also feel too spiritually weary to sustain awareness of the divine with so much vigilance. Maybe during such a season, it would be better to tell the Lord you need a break and to trust in his compassionate understanding. After all, our Creator knows that "we are dust" (Ps 103:14). Legalism does neither the Lord, nor you, any favors.

10. The goal is communion with and deference to God. In the beginning, the outward discipline takes much practice. It may seem artificial. Eventually such prayer becomes involuntary. Instead of "checking out" of what we are doing to "check in" with God, we become as conscious of him as we are of other people in the room, even if he is not the focus of our conversation. The invocation enters our dreams and quiets our actions (Ps 3:5). There is a point, or several points, when we cease striving (Ps 37:7). Our thoughts and emotions shape themselves around the awareness of Christ's presence. Living in prayer enters our rhythm so entirely that rooting it out would be like trying not to breathe. This is preparation for heaven and our eternal communion with the Trinity.

---

[47] Ibid., 31.

Sample the Prayer

Practicing the presence of God is uniquely designed to be sampled for only a few minutes each day or once a week. Steps 1, 3, 5, and 6 above can be increased or decreased to suit the time and energy you have. If even these seem too prohibitive a goal, choose the shower as your selected space (step 8). As you scrub, consider pausing to turn your thoughts to God and resting with him for an extra moment. The advantage of the shower is that most of the usual intrusions will not interrupt you there.

Practice Together

As both Brother Lawrence and Frank Laubach note, it is no easy task to maintain the level of awareness of God that they advocate. For some of us, maintaining that degree of awareness of the people in a small room is difficult enough. Sharing the practice of the presence of God with a spiritual friend or group can be a tremendous encouragement on a day-to-day or week-by-week level.

Knowing that someone else is trying to seek God in the same way you are will prompt you not to give up when you become discouraged and will provide a sympathetic ear when you need to talk about your struggles. Often, when you feel stuck in your own practice, someone else in your group will be able to see your need from a different angle and suggest ideas that you would not have thought of on your own. Regularly reporting on one another's progress, sharing victories, praying for each other's successes, and picking each other up when you stumble, helps maintain momentum and renew joy in the practice.

Furthermore, if your fellow practitioners join you in other activities—shopping, apple-picking, painting the house, going to movies—then you will have opportunities to share the practice itself, rather than simply reporting on it to one another. For example, you might choose a prompt such as announcements from the public address system during an afternoon at the mall (step 3) or play the game of minutes together over dinner (step 5). Take care not to trivialize your references to or rest stops with God, but with intention join in turning to him. Eventually you will notice that God makes his way into your conversations and your silences much more organically.

Deepening your connection with God will work in reverse to deepen your connections with those brothers and sisters who share your practice of the presence. The relationships will feed each other over time so that the energy you have expended to maintain ties with God will witness against easily letting go of the ties with one another—in spite of changes in your work, family structure, geographic location, and health. This, too, is a foretaste of the communion we will enjoy in heaven.

Consider

1. When you consider God's investment in the minutia of your life, how do you characterize his involvement? Do you think God "cares" which city you move to, much less what you cook for your dinner? According to Matthew 10:29–31, God notices and values every hair falling from your head. How does this assertion compare with your assumptions

about his involvement? How does it shape how you view presence prayer?

2. How do you usually evaluate your prayer life? What are the benefits to developing a sense of God's presence by regularly observing your prayer habit?

3. When you compare Brother Lawrence's circumstances and experience of prayer with your own, how practical does his plan sound to you? What do you feel about a ten-year commitment to praying like this? What might motivate you to practice the presence of God in spite of its demands?

4. What are some regular events, chores, visual stimuli, or auditory signals that might function as prompts for you to check in with Jesus? Where in your day do you have the alone-time that might be most conducive to beginning such a plan?

5. What obstacles to this discipline can you envision? How might you overcome them? What plan can you make with your spiritual friend or group to receive help and encouragement when you encounter weariness, defeat, or the temptation to give up?

Study Further

"Brother Lawrence: An Habitual Sense of God's Presence." Pages 369–375 in *Devotional Classics: Selected Readings for Individuals and Groups, revised and expanded.* Edited by Richard J. Foster and James Bryan Smith. New York: HarperSanFrancisco, 2005.

Brother Lawrence. *The Practice of the Presence of God, Revised Edition.* Translated by Robert J. Edmonson. Edited by Hal M. Helms. Orleans, Mass.: Paraclete, 1985.

Foster, Richard J. "Unceasing Prayer." Pages 124–27 in *Prayer: Finding the Heart's True Home.* New York: HarperSanFrancisco, 1992.

"Frank Laubach: Opening Windows to God." Pages 101–107 in *Devotional Classics: Selected Readings for Individuals and Groups, revised and expanded.* Edited by Richard J. Foster and James Bryan Smith. New York: HarperSanFrancisco, 2005.

Laubach, Frank C. *Letters by a Modern Mystic.* Syracuse, N. Y.: New Reader's, 1955.

Wolpert, Daniel. "Journaling: Writing What God Shows Us." Pages 101–112 and 183–84 in *Creating a Life with God: The Call of Ancient Prayer Practices.* Nashville, Tenn.: Upper Room, 2003.

Extemporaneous Prayer
SPENER'S INSISTENCE ON PRAYER, NOT POLITICS

Extemporaneous prayer is spontaneous and usually non-formulaic verbal praise, confession, thanksgiving, and/or petition that we offer to God in silence or out loud.

IDEALLY, IMPROMPTU prayer allows us to talk to our Creator intimately and comfortably, like an innocent child (Matt 6:6, 8–9). However, many of us have grown up in traditions that either never prayed or employed rote prayers and recitations. Others of us feel so at ease with extemporaneous prayer that we downplay the magnitude of the One to whom we are speaking (Amos 5:23–24).

Philip Jacob Spener (1635–1705) saw a trend toward the latter among the early Lutheran churches he pastored. Reformation controversies over doctrine and religious wars had bogged down the unfettered link to God, which Martin Luther had advocated a century before. The agenda-laden pronouncements of the new church had little to do with holiness in everyday life. Instead of theological and political debate, Spener sought moral and spiritual change for his congregation.

He started a small group that met in his home to discuss the Sunday sermon, study the Bible, and pray. He preached new birth (John 3:3–8), a personal Christian experience (John 15:14), and cultivation of the Christian virtues (Jas 2:26). He published these ideas in *Pia Desideria* ("pious longings," 1675). Practitioners became known as Pietists.

Spener and the Pietists sought reform in the larger church through reform of the inner person. If motives were holy, they argued, then outward corruption would be swept away, replaced by good works. Spener encouraged people to "lay the right foundation in the heart," because "what does not proceed from this foundation is mere hypocrisy." "Work," he told them, "on what is inward—awaken love of God and neighbor through suitable means—and only then . . . act accordingly."[48] One of these suitable means was spontaneous prayer. "It is [not] enough," he said, "to pray outwardly with our mouth, but true prayer, and the best prayer, occurs in the inner man, and it either breaks forth in words or remains in the soul, yet God will find and hit upon it."[49]

Furthermore, he insisted that everyone, not just the clergy, the educated, or persons of means, was responsible to God and to the church to be a person of prayer. "Every Christian is bound," he wrote, "to offer himself and what he has—his prayer." And "with the grace that is given him, to . . . pray for all."[50]

Forty years later, his godson the count of Zinzendorf established a village on his land for religious refugees, many of them Pietists. This community devoted itself to prayer and Bible study in small groups. They held one another

---

[48] Philip Jacob Spener, *Pia Desideria* (1675; trans. Theodore G. Tappert; Seminar Editions; ed. Theodore G. Tappert; repr. Philadelphia: Fortress, 1964), 116–17.
[49] Ibid., 117.
[50] Ibid., 94.

accountable to living out their faith in obedience, hoping to continue reforms of the young Lutheran church from within. They studied the Bible, established orphanages, and sent missionaries to India, Iceland, and America. They met for prayer so regularly and for so many years that the group became known as the Hundred-Year Prayer Meeting.

Their emphasis on everyday people, praying freely and honestly, comes down to us through the Wesleyan revivals and the Great Awakening. These in turn became spiritual streams with which we are familiar today. Methodist, Holiness, Pentecostal, Fundamentalist, and Evangelical traditions all emphasize extemporaneous prayer.

Some of us are new to prayer without form. Speaking to God the same way we talk to friends and family may feel disrespectful. Our language may seem stilted, silly, or uncomfortable. We may doubt our right to address God or our ability to find words that express what we mean. For us, the transition into extemporaneous prayer may be gentler if we permit some level of formality in the beginning, such as sticking to a prayer guide. As we follow these leads, eventually our own prayers come to mind more easily and the hope that God hears without judging our performance overcomes our awkwardness (1 Sam 1:14–17).

For others this method of prayer has become so habituated that we pay only partial attention to the conversation we are having with God. We may tick through prayer lists without asking God what he thinks and without entering a waiting posture for his answer. We forget whom we are talking to (Job 40:6–9). If we fail to open ourselves to him, hope in his power to answer and his willingness to forgive is sucked away (Ps 51:1–2; Rom 8:25–26).

We may need to break the flow of extemporaneous prayer and examine what we are doing to renew its power as a spiritual discipline. Have you ever played the "what are you thinking?" game where you are obliged to say whatever was in your head at the moment you were asked? It can be surprising to discover your intersection of ideas or train of thought. In a similar fashion, observing the mechanics of prayer and how we sound when speaking with God allows us to hear old praying and notice its answers in a new way. Then with intention we can reengage the meaningful conversation to which God calls us and lead others in calling out to him (Deut 4:27, 29–31).

Practice

1. Begin where you are. Speaking to God as though he is sitting next to you, tell him what is on your mind.

2. Start now. Do not put it off until everything is in order. There is no need to prepare, to become a better person first, to speak in appropriate tones or formal language, to get your theology straight, to go to a holy place, or to change yourself or your circumstances.

3. Be honest with God. He is your Creator. He sees in you the "division of soul and spirit, joints and marrow" (Heb 4:12 RSV). He knows your secrets, whether or not you reveal them to yourself, to others, or to him. Attempting to hide from him only wastes *your* time. God has eternity at his

disposal. You have some urgency or you would not be considering prayer. Be sure that he sees and receives you just as you are. He longs for you to come.

4. Some people follow guides such as the ACTS acronym (adoration, confession, thanksgiving, supplication/requests) to prompt them. For example, for adoration they ask themselves, "What quality or characteristic of God do I want to rejoice over?" Then they turn their third-person statement into a second-person address: "I'm glad God is a merciful god even though he's also demanding," becomes "I'm glad you love me even though you also seem pretty demanding sometimes." (See also Practice Together below.)

Others use prayers in Scripture as templates for their own prayers. For example, where the Lord's Prayer (Matt 6:9–13) reads "Our Father," they ask themselves which of God's many names fits their sense of him and use that instead of "Father." Some of his names from Scripture include:

- I AM (Exod 3:14)
- Advocate (1 John 2:1)
- Alpha and Omega (Rev 1:8)
- Commander (Josh 5:14)
- Counselor (Isa 9:6)
- Healer (Exod 15:26)
- Holy One (Acts 3:14)
- King (Zech 14:9)
- Life (John 14:6)
- Light (Isa 60:1)

- Pioneer (Heb 2:10; 12:2)
- Provider (Ps 68:10)
- Redeemer (Jer 50:34)
- Rock (Gen 49:24)
- Savior (1 Tim 2:3)
- Servant (Phil 2:7)
- Shepherd (1 Pet 5:4)
- Teacher (Job 36:22)
- The Way (John 14:6)

When it says, "Thy Kingdom come," they think about the small bit of God's kingdom they need in their own work, family, or school and ask for that. For example, "Help my mother make good choices about the men she brings home," or "Transform my job into a place of integrity."

5. Consider offering to God issues outside yourself. What is most important to you right now? Perhaps your friends or family have a need or there is an issue at your work, apartment, or school? What one request or praise would you like to pray for your small group, your church, its ministers, committees, or services? Could you lift your own country, state, or city to God in thanks or petition? Maybe a government leader or a political difficulty will come to mind. Is there a country that you would like God to help today? Perhaps it was in the news. Perhaps it is the home country of someone you know from church or work.

6. Consider issues of your inner person. What do you long for? Can you offer that hope to God? What saddens,

angers, wearies, or cheers you? How would you like God to involve himself in those circumstances? For what do you feel guilt or shame? Can you tell this to God? Can you allow him to wash it away and give you strength and wisdom for making amends? Where in your life have you seen God's blessings? Can you thank him for those?

7. When you are finished, wait for a moment. Prayer is conversation. Allow God to respond. He does not always speak in an audible voice like someone on the other end of the telephone, but he does respond. Listen for that. Look for it. What picture arises in your mind's eye? What word or song repeats in your head? Could this be part of his answer?

8. Make a written note of how your conversation progressed. Share how your prayer developed. If there seemed to be a response immediately or as you listened throughout the day, write that down or share it with a friend. Some people keep short notes on a 3x5 card in their pocket. When they say something to God, they write a two-word summary. Similarly, when an answer or part of an answer presents, they note that, whether it is a phrase from Scripture, the moral of a TV show, or something a friend says. At the end of the day they look through the conversation, reminding themselves of the themes and being encouraged that God was present with them.

9. Many people designate a half hour or more, sometime during the day, to read the Bible and to pray, but find a

never-ending series of interruptions thwarts their efforts. One way they limit outside interruptions and keep themselves on track is to write that half hour into a date book or PDA. Something about the date-book lends cultural legitimacy to the practice of prayer. If someone asks for a meeting during that time, they simply work around their "quiet time" as they would any other scheduling conflict.

Sample the Prayer

If this level of discipline seems too much to achieve right now, consider picking a regular point in the day when you will stop for one minute, ask God's help for one thing you need that day and thank him for one thing that you appreciate. It would probably be best to choose a minute that is likely to be less hectic, not during the morning rush to get out the door, for example.

Practice Together

If there are others praying with you, remember that they are joining you in what you say. You are speaking to God on behalf of a group.

If praying aloud in the presence of other people is too intimidating in the beginning, consider writing down your silent prayers and then telling one another what you prayed.

Or think through the topics your prayer will cover ahead of time. When you are with a small group of people, this often occurs naturally as people share needs or reasons for being thankful. Alternatively, the group may choose to plunge into prayer, each lifting up the needs he or she is

A adoration
C confession
T thanksgiving
S supplication

aware of while the others add their silent or verbal agreement. Often people signal this agreement by saying "amen" during and/or at the end of your prayer. This means "it's true" or "let it be true," or may it be so.

Sometimes groups add structure to their prayers by following the ACTS acronym (see above). During the adoration period, members limit their prayers to praises of God and his character. During confession, members ask God to remove sin, either their own or that of the larger group. When it comes time for thanksgiving, members express their appreciation for what God has done. Supplication is often easiest, for we are most accustomed to calling out for help when we are in need. As they move through each section, groups focus on that sort of prayer only, giving each one time to speak what is in her heart before moving on. One person takes responsibility for shifting to the next section when the group reaches a lull or when the allotted time expires.

When the group is large enough that you need to stand so that all can hear you pray, you can think through topics on your own ahead of time. Even experienced public prayers lose track, repeat filler words ("we just pray," "thank you for this day," etc.), and feel nervous. They may simply make a mental note of petitions, praises, and reasons for thanks, or they may jot themselves a written note. Some type out the full prayer to organize their thoughts even though they do not intend to read directly from the script.

If you are concerned about the undue formality of typing out your prayer, consider the entire process—from your initial thoughts to your spoken word—as your prayer.

Invite the Holy Spirit to guide your words and to receive even your preparation. If you worry that practice eliminates spontaneity, make a list that you wish to cover, but allow your spoken prayer to flow extemporaneously as the Lord leads.

Even though others are listening to you, remember that you are all addressing God. He is the audience. This is not the place to lecture him or others on a theological topic or pet peeve.

Air requests of your own with prudence and ask permission before revealing in public what others have shared in private. God handles everything we place before him with perfect care, but those listening may not be able or ready to act on what they hear with mercy and grace.

Have compassion on those you are leading. Remember that some of them have short attention-spans, feel fidgety from aches and pains, or are new to sustained periods of prayer. There are seasons when your group will endure long talks with God, pouring out everything inside. At other times, the group may share briefly with God, trusting that he understands without an extended explanation. Know the difference, and limit your praying time accordingly.

Consider

1. What are some of the challenges to praying spont-aneously or without more planning than a simple list of needs and praises? What are some of the benefits?

2. What do you like most about praying aloud in this fashion? What is most difficult?

3. Some traditions emphasize spontaneous prayers, while others employ tried and true liturgies. Some encourage members of the group to respond verbally to others' prayers as they are being prayed. Others focus on an orderly approach to God. What sort of traditions are you accustomed to? How does the conversational prayer experience change your view of God or your individual relationship to him?

4. If spontaneous prayer is new to you or someone you know, it may be difficult to speak naturally. What are some steps you could take to relieve the discomfort of talking with God in this conversational fashion?

Study Further

Blythe, Theresa A. "Prayer Partnering." Pages 125–127 and 201–2 in *50 Ways to Pray: Practices from Many Traditions and Times*. Nashville, Tenn.: Abingdon, 2006.

Foster, Richard J. "Simple Prayer." Pages 7–15 in *Prayer: Finding the Heart's True Home*. New York: HarperSan-Francisco, 1992.

Guenther, Margaret. Pages 46–60 in *The Practice of Prayer*. Volume 4 in *The New Church's Teaching Series*. Cambridge, Mass.: Cowley, 1998.

Mayfield, Sue. Pages 62–64 and 74–75 in *Exploring Prayer*. Peabody, Mass.: Hendrickson, 2007.

Spener, Philip Jacob. *Pia Desideria*. Seminar Editions. Edited by Theodore G. Tappert. Translated by Theodore G. Tappert. 1675. Reprinted by Philadelphia: Fortress, 1964.

Stookey, Laurence Hull. *Let the Whole Church Say Amen! A Guide for Those Who Pray in Public.* Nashville, Tenn.: Abingdon, 2001.

Thurston, Bonnie. "*Oratio:* Praying with Words." Pages 24–53 in *For God Alone: A Primer on Prayer.* Notre Dame, Ind.: University of Notre Dame Press, 2009.

Prayer of Examen

Examen prayer is the Holy Spirit's application to our lives of scriptural teachings or descriptions of holiness in order to determine where we lack and/or succeed in living a holy life.

ODD THOUGH this may sound, freedom is the reason we allow the dark spaces in our souls to be exposed to the light of God's examination. Instinct argues that while the darkness is terrifying, exposure to the light is painful, risky, and ultimately futile. Martin Luther, however, discovered that when he allowed *God* to shine the light, it was fear that fled from Luther instead of Luther failing in his attempts to flee from the darkness (John 3:17–21).

Martin Luther (1483–1546) was a typical Catholic of the sixteenth century, except for his acute and debilitating fear of judgment. His anxiety was compounded when, one night as he walked home, a bolt of lightning either struck him or struck close enough to knock him over. He cried out to St. Anne in terror, pledging to become a monk, if only he were saved from the hellfire.

To keep his vow, he joined a strict order of Augustinians, and in spite of his dislike for monastic life, carried out the oath—if for no other reason than to ease his fear. Not only did he submit to his superiors, studying for a doctorate in theology and becoming a priest, he also practiced monastic disciplines excessively. Yet he could find no peace, no sense of assurance concerning his position before the holy Judge.

Then, sometime between 1513 and 1517, as he prepared and taught classes in Psalms, Romans, and Galatians, Paul's phrase, "the just shall live by faith" (Rom 1:17 KJV; see also Hab 2:4) set him free. He finally understood that God received him because of Christ's trustworthy work on the cross, and not because of Luther's own works, worthy or unworthy. His discovery became a foundation for the Reformation.

Luther's new perspective on God established a new manner of coping with his sin. Instead of the self-flagellation he had rigorously practiced in order to avoid the deceit of self-justification, he trusted the Lord to reveal and reclaim what was not right in his life. As he studied Scripture, he waited on the Spirit to apply the word specifically to him, nudging him in the direction he should turn.

Commenting on this approach to conviction and confession, called "examen," Luther writes, "There is no better mirror in which to see your need than simply the Ten Commandments, in which you will find what you lack and what you should seek. If, therefore, you find in yourself a weak faith, small hope, and little love toward God, . . . these you shall earnestly lay before God, lament and ask for help, and with all confidence expect help, and believe that you are heard and shall obtain help and mercy."[51]

---

[51] Martin Luther, *A Treatise on Good Works Together with the Letter of Dedication* (1520), n.p. [cited 19 June 2008]. Online: www.theologywebsite.com/etext/luther_goodworks.shtml.

Considering the big picture Jesus painted regarding the possibilities for sin, Luther probably saw the Ten Commandments as more than a simple check-list of ethical dos and don'ts. Matthew 5:21–24 suggests that the command against murder was broken when someone was at fault in a dispute and failed to attempt reconciliation. According to Jesus, a lustful look alone ranked with committing adultery (Matt 5:27–28). The rich young ruler vouched that he had obeyed all ten laws religiously, but Jesus directed the man to care for the poor and to follow the Master if he wanted to practice them as God desired (Matt 19:17–21). Jesus himself "broke" traditional concepts of Sabbath because he understood that true Sabbath-keeping also had to do with healing (Mark 3:1–5; John 5:2–16).

From his days of fear, Luther knew that there was more to obedience than legalistic observance. He had already tried legalism to no avail. He came to believe that God already knew every hidden corner of his life. His new freedom was found by inviting God into those corners to sweep them clean (Ps 139:1, 23–24), instead of trying to tidy them up himself.

Like Luther, we may question whether we have done enough. The inner critic plagues us with our imperfect work. The shoulder devil prods incessantly at our personal failings. Believing in God's mercy is not the problem; believing in his mercy for *me* is the difficulty. Practicing the prayer of examen trains believers to hear the Spirit's gently convicting voice rather than inner PA systems that blare self-condemnation. Granting God the right to root out sin frees us from the struggle to master that which is too big for us to do in the first place (John 8:32).

For other believers, "live free!" may already be our motto. We struggle to focus on the inner darkness and how it leaks out onto other people. Acknowledging complicated consequences of sin and "fallenness" seems to steal our opportunities to play in the light. Even "making amends," the ninth step in twelve-step recovery programs, smacks of making a big deal. We would rather make people laugh. The prayer of examen grants us a way to follow Jesus into a light that fills our empty places (Job 33:29–30), and it opens the path to a mercy that is sweeter than honey from the rock (Ps 81:16).

Practice

1. Invite God to search the depths of your heart as you meditate on the Ten Commandments found in Exodus 20:1–20. Ask him for insight into how the truth in Scripture and your own experience have intersected.

2. You may wish to hold up other Scriptures as a mirror for your soul. Some suggestions include the wisdom literature of Proverbs and Ecclesiastes, the Psalms, the Beatitudes (Matt 5:1–12), Paul's New Life in Christ (Col 3), or the Well-Pleasing Service (Heb 13).

3. Read slowly, pausing at each sentence or verse to listen for anything that stands out. Perhaps there is an area of your life that you would like God to examine—your use of time, your relationship with your coworkers, the books you

read, etc. Perhaps you will invite him to look through a particular period, your day or your week. Think through your thoughts, feelings, and actions in the context of the passage. How did they draw you to God? To self? How were they like or unlike the picture of God that the reading paints? How has God been at work? What seemingly ordinary things might God have been using for his own purposes? How did you respond?

4. If you find your mind wandering or trying to dredge up remorse without conviction (Matt 6:7–8), perhaps it is time to move on to the next sentence or verse (see pp 108–109 for suggestions on how to deal with distractions).

5. When something not quite right comes to light, avoid the urge to defend yourself. Instead take responsibility for what is wrong and ask God to purify you. On the other hand, avoid the urge to punish yourself. Trust that you will receive God's mercy (Eph 2:4–5).

6. God's Spirit encourages as much as he convicts. As you practice the prayer of examen, do not forget to sit still for his smile. When something is shown to you that falls in line with the commands, do not diminish it. Thank God for this evidence of his work through you and for allowing you to participate in his plan (Jer 9:23–24).

7. If it is difficult to hear his voice pointing out matters for celebration or confession in your life because your own inner voice drowns him out, begin by listening for *his*

characteristics or actions instead of your own. What does God reveal about himself as you read through the Commandments?

8. Write down your confession to God, both the truth about yourself and the truth about him. Make sure to note the whole truth: his holiness, which cannot be trespassed against, as well as his love that redeems you with mercy. If you have felt a nudge concerning an action you might take, a word you might offer, or a new perspective you might adopt, write that down, too. When you are done meditating through the passage, read what you have written. Thank him for his work. Offer all that you have discovered about yourself to all that you know to be true of God. The goal is not to journey into yourself and stay there, but to journey through yourself to the heart of God.[52] Yield to his righteousness and mercy and wait.

9. Finally, do not forget that when you leave the mirror, you can leave with confidence and peace that he has shown you all you need concern yourself with today (1 Cor 2:10; Phil 3:13–14).

Sample the Prayer

If you only have a few minutes to spend with God today, contemplate one commandment (or one verse), instead of all ten. Trust God to coordinate the days and the

---

[52] Richard J. Foster, *Prayer: Finding the Heart's True Home* (New York: HarperSanFrancisco, 1992), 32.

verses by his unsearchable sense of timing. If the time you set aside for looking into his Ten Commandments "mirror" is too long to endure, start with five minutes and add one minute a day. You might also reserve it for seasons of evaluation during Lent, Communion, or a spiritual retreat or you might apply it to a particular meeting, conversation, or product-development in which you participated.

Practice Together

Practicing examen as a group requires discipline, gentleness, humility, and trust. After all, it is often easier to acknowledge our faults to God, who assures us of his forgiveness (1 John 1:9), than to the human whom we have sinned against. Furthermore, it is possible for members to abuse this practice, breaking confidentiality or using confessed weakness to manipulate others. Groups should consider the strength of internal relationships and trustworthiness of individual members before asking this of one another.

On the other hand, an exercise in honest group examen can yield unparalleled depth and freedom to your community life as you confess your sins to one another and receive forgiveness and healing (Jas 5:16). Groups who are new to one another can start by practicing step 7 above. From there, groups may eventually explore accountability with one another, confessing weaknesses or sins for which individuals would welcome prayer support and other help. Groups who have made longer lasting commitments to one another may dig deeper for the sake of group unity by examining sins against the group or darkness between individuals within the circle.

Begin by inviting God and his Son's sacrifice to set the example for your group (Phil 2:5–8), and ask the Holy Spirit to direct your words and your interactions with one another. Give everyone a portion of the passage to read aloud. After each one reads, wait in silence before God. Then share what he has brought to mind for confession.

Perhaps only the one who has taken his turn reading will share, trusting that the Lord guides even the distribution of the verses to the exact person who needs that verse that day. Or perhaps everyone who has heard something for that particular commandment will share. Set the ground rules ahead of time in order to avoid adding confusion to a season of prayer that may be intense already.

If confession of sin is made, and the one who has been sinned against is present, grant that person a chance to forgive the offender (Matt 5:23–24). If deeper reconciliation or restitution seems necessary, the group should come alongside the two in need (Phil 4:2–3).

Whether or not immediate reconciliation is possible, someone should answer the confession of sin with a confession of the truth about God from his promises. For example if someone recognizes and admits a tendency toward self-deception, another can remember aloud that God has granted an "antidote" to the difficulty of remembering the truth about ourselves: looking into the law of freedom and obeying that (Jas 1:22–25).

End the season of examen together by thanking God for his mercy and agreeing to receive the liberty that comes with that mercy.

Consider

1. "The just shall live by faith" (Rom 1:17 KJV) is a foundational phrase in the Reformation. Who are "the just"? What does it mean for them to "live by faith"? How does this theology influence your feeling of confidence under the scrutiny of this kind of prayer?

2. In John 8:32, Jesus says, "You will know the truth, and the truth will make you free" (RSV). What truth does he mean? How is there freedom in hearing the truth? If Jesus is love, how is it loving for Jesus to tell you truths about the darkness within yourself?

3. Focusing on long-suppressed fears or habits of sin can be a little dangerous. On the other hand, ignoring these things can be dangerous, too. Do you see either tendency in yourself? If so, how have you dealt with this in the past? How might the prayer of examen provide you with a different option? How can you avoid your default tendency while practicing examen?

4. God calls communities of believers, not just individuals. He convicts and encourages his people as a group, too. What special direction(s) or theme(s) would your particular group need to practice this prayer in unity?

Study Further

Blythe, Theresa A. Pages 58–61 and 167–70 in *50 Ways to Pray: Practices from Many Traditions and Times*. Nashville, Tenn.: Abingdon, 2006.

Foster, Richard J. "The Prayer of Examen." Pages 27–35 in *Prayer: Finding the Heart's True Home.* New York: HarperSanFrancisco, 1992.

"Martin Luther: Praying in Faith." Pages 115–20 in *Devotional Classics: Selected Readings for Individuals and Groups, revised and expanded.* Edited by Richard J. Foster and James Bryan Smith. New York: HarperSanFrancisco, 2005.

Luther, Martin. *A Simple Way to Pray (. . . for Master Peter the Barber).* 1535. Cited 12 June 2008. Online: www.hope-aurora.org/docs/ASimpleWaytoPray.pdf.

Luther, Martin. *A Treatise on Good Works Together with the Letter of Dedication.* 1520. Evanston, Ill.: Theology Website, 2005. No pages. Cited 19 June 2008. Online: www.theology website.com/etext/luther_goodworks.shtml.

Skehan, James W. "Format for the Practice of Christian Insight Meditation (CIM)." Page 12 in *Place Me With Your Son: Ignatian Spirituality in Everyday Life.* Washington, D.C.: Georgetown University Press, 1991.

Wolpert, Daniel. "The Examen: God in Day-to-Day Life." Pages 75–87 and 180–81 in *Creating a Life with God: The Call of Ancient Prayer Practices.* Nashville, Tenn.: Upper Room, 2003.

Liturgical Prayer
CRANMER'S TRIED AND TRUE LANGUAGE

Liturgical prayer is ritual verbal praise, confession, thanksgiving, and/or petition that we offer to God, often in the company of other pray-ers.

LITURGY IN PRAYER is as old as the *Shema* (meaning "hear"), a Hebrew summons to confess the nature of God: "Hear, O Israel, the Lord your God is one" (Deut 6:4–5). Moses commanded the Israelites to repeat the *Shema* regularly (6:6–9) in order to fix the call firmly in their hearts. Liturgical prayer can also be found in many of the Psalms that were used in Temple worship. Psalm 67 is a recognizable example with its refrain, "Let the peoples praise thee, O God; let all the peoples praise thee!" Similarly, every verse in the antiphonal Psalm 136 concludes with the response "for his mercy endures forever." The most famous New Testament liturgy, the *Our Father*, acts as both a specific prayer and a template for how to pray (Matt 6:9–13).

Liturgies from both the Old and New Testaments continued to be used in the early church even as new prayers developed and were codified (Acts 2:42). By AD 1220, the Roman Catholic church was collecting service books from across England to standardize their prayers and practices. The resulting liturgies multiplied until Thomas

Cranmer began his reformation revisions.[53]

Cranmer was born in 1489 to a wealthy farmer. His keen mind and conservative,[54] penetrating disposition suited him to the life of an academic. He rose so quickly in the university system and the church that King Henry VIII took notice of him and sent him to the Continent as an envoy. In 1533, Henry recalled Cranmer from his diplomatic duties and reformation studies to consecrate him Archbishop of Canterbury.

At this time Henry had already begun proceedings to force the annulment of his first marriage, since it had not produced a male heir, but the English church had yet to break completely with Rome. Nevertheless, cracks between the English government and Roman authority had widened sufficiently to bother the cautious Cranmer. Consecration as archbishop included swearing an oath of obedience to the pope, and he thought this would conflict with his obedience to the crown, so he made it known that he was taking the oath only as a formality. He would neither oppose the crown, nor limit his pursuit of reformation in the Church of England.[55]

A formal Act of Supremacy, proclaiming that Henry outranked the pope, was finally issued at the end of 1534. Cranmer took advantage of the political move to begin reforming the services and prayers of the English church.

---

[53] G. Eric Lane, "Cranmer's Prayer Book and Its Influence," in *The Reformation of Worship: 1989 Westminster Conference Papers* (Surrey, England, 1990), 17.

[54] Marcus L. Loane, "Thomas Cranmer," in *Masters of the English Reformation* (1954; repr. Carlisle, Penn.: Banner of Truth Trust, 2005), 257.

[55] Ibid., 232–33.

Ten years later, Henry ordered him to write prayers in the English language for the king's armies to recite as they went into battle. These were the first published portions of a new English liturgy.[56]

Cranmer is best known for his lifelong work of filtering, translating, simplifying, and unifying the church service into one work that became known as the *Book of Common Prayer*. From older service books, he rooted out content that was neither Scripture-based nor supported by the early church fathers. He wrote reformed prayers and practices in the vernacular, simplified instructions for worship services so that common people could follow along, and combined a variety of traditions into one.[57]

Ironically, the conservative populace was outraged by this switch to English language services, perhaps because they felt that English was too common, not beautiful enough for worship.[58] Or perhaps the use of their own language implied greater participation in their faith than could be expected back when religion was performed in Latin.[59] Furthermore, instead of making a private confession to the priest before the service, people now spoke aloud a unified confession directly to God, asking "Lord have mercy" after the Ten Commandments were read.[60]

In the preface to the 1549 edition of the English service

---

[56] Lane, "Cranmer's Prayer Book," 18.

[57] Ibid., 18–20.

[58] Ibid., 23–25.

[59] Jasper Ridley, *Thomas Cranmer* (Oxford: Clarendon, 1962), 288.

[60] Lane, "Cranmer's Prayer Book," 18, 21.

book, Cranmer explained, "Whereas St Paul would have such language spoken to the people in the church, as they might understand and have profit by hearing the same [1 Cor 14:5–12]; the service in this Church of England (these many years) hath been read in Latin to the people, which they understood not; so that they have heard with their ears only; and their hearts, spirit, and mind, have not been edified thereby."[61]

In 1552, under the authority of Henry's son, a final version called the *Second Prayer Book of Edward VI* was issued. The book specified both the methods and the words to be used in services of worship, feast days, consecrations, marriages, baptisms, burials, and ordinary days throughout the church calendar. Cranmer wrote many of the prayers himself and translated others from ancient sources. His combination of words and styles from both the Germanic and the Latin roots of English resulted in memorable phrases—"meet, right, and our bounden duty"—that continue to appeal to a wide range of participants. His ability to convey spiritual experience and deep theology with drama and ease for unified recitation has caused these written prayers to flourish for centuries.[62]

Anglican and Episcopal traditions continue to employ an edition of the *Book of Common Prayer* similar to Edward's. Other high church traditions, such as Roman Catholicism

---

[61] Thomas Cranmer, preface to *The First Book of Edward VI* (1549), quoted in William Reed Huntington, *A Short History of the Book of Common Prayer* (1893), n.p. [cited 24 June 2009]. Online: www.justus.anglican.org/resources/bcp/short_history_BCP.htm.

[62] Lane, "Cranmer's Prayer Book," 23–25.

and Lutheranism, also enjoy tried and true collections of prayer. Liturgical prayer in low church traditions can be heard in the repetition of Scripture songs and in the "amen," "yes Jesus," and "uh-hmm" of call and response preaching.

At its best, liturgical prayer answers our need to pray "thy kingdom come" as something besides a disappointed concession. It broadens our perspective,[63] teaching us to pray beyond our small scope. When we cannot find words to pray because of chaos in our world or in our minds, liturgical prayer supplies them. When we mistrust our own abilities to say what we mean or to hear the Lord speaking back, liturgical prayer provides the tried and true language of our great cloud of witnesses (Heb 12:1). If we are like Cranmer, cautious and careful, perhaps afraid our prayers are trivial and unworthy for lack of knowledge, liturgical prayers offer the comfort of standing the test of time, while expressing profound truths of our own experience.

Cranmer was cautious to the end. Scholars debate whether he was a political chameleon, surviving several very different governments by accommodating the powers that be, or a skilled diplomat, bringing extreme factions of the Reformation and Roman Catholicism together through meticulous scholarship and patient loyalty. His work ended when Mary, Henry's only surviving child with his first wife, came to the throne bent on blotting out all reforms and returning English worship to Rome. Thomas Cranmer was

[63] Richard J. Foster, *Prayer: Finding the Heart's True Home* (New York: HarperSanFrancisco, 1992), 107–108.

forced to recant his revisions or be burned alive. Caught between his oath of obedience to his sovereign and his beliefs,[64] he renounced his beliefs. But after an agonizing night, he changed his mind. Instead of reading his refutation, he publicly begged God's forgiveness. He was burned at the stake on March 21, 1556, at the age of 66. His prayers of petition survive, and thrive, to this day.[65]

Practice

1. Choose a liturgical prayer to practice. Two prayers from the *Book of Common Prayer* are printed here.[66] They are known as "suffrages" or short intercessory prayers that are usually spoken in a series. You may be aware of similar, often repeated prayers from your church. Some churches, for example, lay out Psalms at the back of their hymnals for antiphonal reading. Other collections of prayers are listed in the Study Further section below.

Rite II: Evening Prayer, Suffrage A

Show us your mercy, O Lord;
> *And grant us your salvation.*

Clothe your ministers with righteousness;
> *Let your people sing with joy.*

Give peace, O Lord, in all the world;
> *For only in you can we live in safety.*

---

[64] Loane, "Thomas Cranmer," 288–89.

[65] Ibid., 300.

[66] *The Book of Common Prayer and the Administration of the Sacraments and Other Rites and Ceremonies of the Church Together with The Psalter or Psalms of David: According to the Use of the Episcopal Church* (1789; repr. New York: Church Hymnal Corporation, n.d.), 121–22.

Lord, keep this nation under your care;
> *And guide us in the way of justice and truth.*

Let your way be known upon earth;
> *Your saving health among all nations.*

Let not the needy, O Lord, be forgotten;
> *Nor the hope of the poor be taken away.*

Create in us clean hearts, O God;
> *And sustain us with your Holy Spirit.*

Rite II: Evening Prayer, Suffrage B

That this evening may be holy, good, and peaceful,
> *We entreat you, O Lord.*

That your holy angels may lead us in paths of peace and goodwill,
> *We entreat you, O Lord.*

That we may be pardoned and forgiven for our sins and offenses,
> *We entreat you, O Lord.*

That there may be peace to your Church and to the whole world,
> *We entreat you, O Lord.*

That we may depart this life in your faith and fear, and not be condemned before the great judgment seat of Christ,
> *We entreat you, O Lord.*

That we may be bound together by your Holy Spirit in the communion of all your saints, entrusting one another and all our life to Christ,
> *We entreat you, O Lord.*

2. Read the words of the written prayer to yourself slowly. Do not skim. Especially if you are familiar with the prayer, discipline yourself to listen to it anew. Avoid "heap[ing] up empty phrases" in your mind (Matt 6:7 RSV). If you do not feel like praying or know what to pray, permit the words to speak for you. Allow yourself to own the prayer. Let the words or phrases express the yearnings of your own heart, but do not concern yourself if they seem irrelevant to your immediate needs. Hear the whole truth that you are speaking to God.

3. Mouth the prayer to yourself or whisper it softly. Listen for the words that reach beyond your own requests to the life of the community of which you are a part. Consider others on whose behalf you speak these words of praise, confession, thanksgiving, or petition.

4. Pray the prayer out loud. Keep a deliberate pace. Resist the temptation to race or to over-focus on accurate intonation and correct emphasis. Embrace your stutters and mispronunciations as part of the music you bring before the Lord. Join your voice with those throughout the ages and around the world who have prayed this prayer.

5. Pause in silence as the ring of the prayer settles. Listen to the echoes in the room or in your mind.

6. Repeat the prayer again. This time focus on the Lord before whom you offer these words. Some people avoid such prayers because they suspect that lack of spontaneity

means they are faking it before God, treating him as less than the Almighty. If you feel this way, consider your participation in the ritual of other ceremonies (baptism, communion, and weddings, for example). When you choose to adopt the forms of a ceremony as your own, you intentionally join your voice with those of the saints around you and who have gone before you. You consent to a formality that has come to signal the awesome presence of the Most High. So, too, can liturgical prayer signal the grandeur of the King to whose throne you draw near together.

7. At the "Amen," pause again to listen.

8. Write down the aspect(s) of the prayer or the praying that spoke for you or your community today or share your insights with a spiritual friend or small group.

9. Notice the words of the prayer returning to you throughout the day or later on when a situation arises to which they pertain.

Sample the Prayer

If repeating this sort of prayer on your own seems laborious, consider visiting a liturgical church to experience the prayer. You might attend an Episcopal, Lutheran, or Catholic church some Sunday morning. Perhaps you could visit such a church while away from your regular practice, on vacation or a business trip. Episcopal churches may offer an early mass in addition to the traditional 11 o'clock service, and Catholic churches often hold a family mass on Saturday afternoons.

Practice Together

Most written prayers are intended for the community of believers. Even when individuals pray alone, they join their voices with those who employ the same words. As with any other group activity, there is comfort and perspective in this unified approach. Indeed, the *Book of Common Prayer* was written first for the purpose of edifying the body of believers. Individual use is only its secondary purpose.

If you are in a group, begin as above, reading the words to yourself and then mouthing or whispering them softly. Pray aloud together, in unison or antiphonally, as the prayer suggests. Listen to the person next to you. Do not concern yourselves with perfect pronunciations, but take a measured pace so you can hear and join with one another. When you finish, listen in silence. Be aware of how God may be responding, what words, phrases, or thoughts are resonating, and how these interact with your group's situation or need. Repeat the prayer, again in unison. This time focus on the Lord to whom you are praying. What aspects of his character or work does the prayer emphasize? Listen in silence for a few moments.

After the silence, you may wish to share with one another what stood out to you as you prayed. Or you may simply move on to the next group activity, resting in the assurance that God has heard your petitions and praises and joins your group as you proceed.

Consider

1. The use of liturgical prayer in church, small groups, or as individuals often generates strong emotions, particularly for those who have prior experience with written prayer or who have received prior teaching about it. What is your history with this sort of prayer? Is it comfortable? Does it feel artificial? If you do have an opinion about it, how did it arise?

2. "High church" refers to churches that are hierarchical in their government and formal in their liturgy, but even churches that shun formality settle into a comfortable rhythm of worship that could be called that particular church's liturgy. Think about your own church or community of faith. What elements are often seen in its style of prayer?

3. Consider your small group's style of praying or your own personal approach to prayer. What benefits might you derive from employing written prayers? What are the drawbacks of this level of formality? What are the advantages or disadvantages of repeating familiar phrases? How does the feel or dynamic change when you try liturgical prayer?

Study Further

Barbee, C. Frederick, and Paul R. M. Zahl. *The Collects of Thomas Cranmer.* Grand Rapids, Mich.: Eerdmans, 1990.

Bennett, Arthur, ed. *The Valley of Vision: A Collection of Puritan Prayers and Devotions.* Carlisle, Penn.: Banner of Truth Trust, 1975.

The Book of Common Prayer and the Administration of the Sacraments and Other Rites and Ceremonies of the Church Together with The Psalter or Psalms of David: According to the Use of the Episcopal Church. 1789. Reprint. New York: Church Hymnal Corporation, n.d.

Foster, Richard J. "Sacramental Prayer." Pages 107–108 in *Prayer: Finding the Heart's True Home*. New York: Harper-SanFrancisco, 1992.

Guenther, Margaret. "Books of Prayers." Pages 72–74 in *The Practice of Prayer*. Volume 4 in *The New Church's Teaching Series*. Cambridge, Mass.: Cowley, 1998.

Lane, G. Eric. "Cranmer's Prayer Book and Its Influence." Pages 17–35 in *The Reformation of Worship: 1989 Westminster Conference Papers*. Surrey, England: Westminster Conference, 1990.

Marcus L. Loane. "Thomas Cranmer." Pages 224–303 in *Masters of the English Reformation*. 1954. Reprint. Carlisle, Penn.: Banner of Truth Trust, 2005.

Northumbria Community. *Celtic Daily Prayer: Prayers and Readings from the Northumbria Community*. New York: HarperOne, 2002.

Imagination Prayer
IGNATIUS' FIVE SENSES OF THE IMAGINATION

Imagination prayer is shared experience with Jesus that is based on stories of Jesus from the Gospels and that draws on our use of empathy and visualization.

IMAGINATION PRAYER is designed to help us experience being with Jesus. The fears and joys Jesus' contemporaries felt were true responses to his personality, his work, and his words (Matt 28:8). Walking with him allowed them to know his presence with intimacy and certainty (Luke 24:32). Ignatius of Loyola began his journey looking for that same encounter with Christ.

Christened Iñigo López (c. 1491–1556), Ignatius was born into a noble family in Basque, on the Spanish side of the border. As a younger son, his career options were limited. Another brother took the church job, so Iñigo entered the military. In 1521, during a French invasion of the city he was defending, a cannonball shattered his leg. His injury healed incorrectly and required surgery to re-break and set the bone and to shave the resulting bulge.

During his long confinement, Iñigo could not find any of the chivalry books he preferred, so he read the only works at hand, a life of Christ and a legends of the saints. Unable to pursue the usual diversions of a military man, he pondered his encounter with death and considered his lifestyle in light of these saints. By the time his leg was healed, he had committed himself to a saint's path (1 Cor 1:2).

He confessed his sins, donated his fine clothes to the poor, and took vows of poverty and chastity. Keeping vigil one night in a chapel, he dedicated even his weapons and his knightly skills to the service of God. For a year, he lived in a Dominican priory as a monk and practiced a severe asceticism, but none of this seemed to minister Jesus' presence to him. Despair and suicide often tempted him instead.

Still, he persevered. Following the saintly life further, he made a pilgrimage to the Holy Land, pledging to remain in Jerusalem as a missionary. However, the mission society that was already there forbade his work, so he began a long trek back to Spain to study. On the way, Iñigo received a vision of the Messiah. This experience comforted him more than any of his previous attempts at obedience. For the rest of his life, he sought to see and hear Jesus during meditation as a source of reassurance.

Iñigo folded all these experiences into his *Spiritual Exercises,* a book that deeply influenced the Catholic Counter-Reformation. The exercises drew on disciplines of meditation, contemplation, prayer, and supervision. They functioned as a tool for conquering selfishness, examining conscience, realigning habits, and making decisions. Initially he offered the exercises to the serfs and the sick to whom he preached on the streets.

This informal preaching and spiritual direction roused Inquisition suspicions, and he was jailed by both of the first two universities that he attended. Eventually, he entered the

University of Paris, where future Protestant Reformer John Calvin was also studying. Now known by his Latin name, Ignatius earned a master of arts in theology and practiced his spiritual disciplines with a small group of close friends. These seven men took vows together to obey the Pope in whatever missionary endeavor he might command, and in 1540 they obtained his permission to establish the Society of Jesus, the Jesuits.

The following method of prayer derives from the *Spiritual Exercises,* "Week Two," which summons us to meditate on gospel accounts of Jesus' birth. Ignatius writes, "it is helpful to pass the five senses of the imagination through . . . contemplation, in the following way: The first point is to see the persons with the sight of the imagination, meditating and contemplating in particular the details about them. . . . The second, to hear with the hearing what they are, or might be, talking about. . . . The third [and fourth], to smell and to taste. . . . The [fifth], to touch with the touch, as for instance, . . . the places where such persons put their feet and sit, always seeing to my drawing profit from [this exercise]."[67]

Like Iñigo, we may long to know Jesus intimately, but prefer action—even good works—or escape to medicate the inner chaos. We would rather do battle for Jesus, than risk being sucked under by uncomfortable emotions that might arise if we sit still with Jesus. Imagination prayer provides a structured foray into the heart (Ps 33:20–21). It

---

[67] "The Spiritual Exercises of St. Ignatius of Loyola" (trans. Elder Mullan; Grand Rapids, Mich.: Christian Classics Ethereal Library, 2005), 32. Cited 1 Aug 2006. Online: www.ccel.org/ccel/ignatius/exercises.html.

engages our social awareness, minimizing emotion for emotion's sake. Instead of losing ourselves in busyness or fantasy, we employ our imaginations to identify with a character from the gospels who knew Jesus and through that empathy discover our own conversations with the Lord (John 16:12–13).

On the other hand, we may find ourselves trapped in our heads or blocked by the hurt of previous human relationships. We gather information as a retreat into the mind's storeroom of ideas. Perhaps we read or ask questions in order to avoid the space in our own hearts designed for people. Instead this Ignatian prayer uses our imaginations to skirt this dominance of the analytical mind. It cracks the parlor door for a gentle Savior, whom we can trust to handle us with care and to fill the emptiness with warmth (Matt 9:36; Rev 3:20). And as we maintain this engagement with him, we add depth and scope to how we share him with those around us.

Practice

1. Pick an action scene from the gospels as a foundation for your prayer. In other words, choose a story in which Jesus is doing something rather than teaching something. Some possible stories include:

- Jesus Heals Two Blind Men (Matt 9:27–31)
- Jesus Walks on Water (Matt 14:22–43)
- Jesus Heals Jairus' Daughter and the Bleeding Woman (Mark 5:21–43)
- A Woman Anoints Jesus (Mark 14:3–9)

- Jesus' Heals in Simon's House (Luke 4:37–41)
- Jesus Goes to the Cross (Luke 23:26–30)
- Jesus Raises Lazarus (John 11:28–44)
- Thomas Believes Jesus Is Alive (John 20:24–29)

2. Read the passage several times. Perhaps once you'll read slowly as if for the first time. Another time through, maybe reading it aloud will help you get the feeling of the whole scene.

3. Invite the Lord to be present with you, to guide and protect as you seek to be with him.

4. Now quiet yourself before God. Some people use techniques like body awareness and breathing to still themselves.

5. Let your imagination work on the gospel scene. Imagine the location. In other words, are you by a lake or on a mountain? What time of day is it? See the people involved. Who is there with Jesus? City folk, farmers, shepherds, the disciples, women, Pharisees, crowds? How do your feet feel? What do you bump into, touch with your hands? What do you smell? What do you taste? What is being said by Jesus and others? What emotions might be in the hearts of various people? What actions are taken by Jesus and others?

6. Put yourself at the scene. Take the place of one of the

characters and see the scene through the eyes of that person. What is he or she feeling? Thinking? Doing?

7. Release your imagination from your inner critic. Your imagined scene need not reproduce first-century Jerusalem with forensic accuracy. Let go of your prayer list. You and God can talk about details of your day later. (See pp 108–109 for suggestions on how to deal with distractions.) The point is neither to see "right," nor to cover everything, but to be with Jesus. Remember that you come to God as a child to his mother. Her presence is sufficient to comfort her child (Ps 131:2). The child does not require her to produce scientific evidence that there is no monster under the bed. In the same way, do not refuse to enjoy Jesus' presence until this form of prayer measures up to whatever criteria your mind may generate (Job 40:2–4; Rom 11:34). Remember that God has redeemed all of your faculties, including your imagination (Luke 5:23–24). More importantly, it is he whom we trust to communicate clearly using whatever method he chooses.

8. On the other hand, do not be consumed and over-whelmed by your emotions. With intention, choose to be "taken in" by your encounter with Jesus without becoming sucked under by the scene. Emotionalism is not the goal in itself. Being together with Jesus, experiencing his presence, is the goal (Luke 10:39).

9. Now "freeze frame." Stay with a particular picture involving yourself and Jesus. Talk to him and listen to what

he says to you. Spend time in his presence. Allow your imagination to serve your faith. Jesus is not here the way you imagine him, but he most assuredly is with you, seeing you, listening to you, speaking to you.

10. Do you come away from the scene with Jesus frustrated, empty, worried, content, eager? Are these actually reflections of how you feel about your daily, *non*-imagined walk with Jesus or about a particular circumstance with which you want him to be involved? When you consider what happens after your scene, as recorded in Scripture, does that change how you think about your encounter? Ignatian prayer is meant to be experiential. Perhaps you simply spent uninterrupted time with him. The purpose is not necessarily to gain new spiritual insights—though these may come—but to deepen your relationship with Jesus.

11. Write down what you have heard, what happened, what you said, and/or what the theme seemed to be, or share this with your small group, prayer partner, or spiritual friend.

Sample the Prayer

When your time for meditation is limited, dwell on only one of the above sensory questions and apply it to only one of the characters in the scene. For example, in the story of Jesus walking on the water, think about whether and how sea-sick Peter felt in the boat because of the waves. How would you feel in that circumstance? Tomorrow, return to the story again and reflect on how the water felt under Peter's feet. Work your way through the story slowly, asking yourself how you relate (or do not) to that character's experience with Jesus.

Practice Together

If you would like to practice imagination prayer as a group, there are several approaches you may take. The first is a guided individual experience, which members share and process afterwards. In the second, members act out the story together, simultaneously role-playing—the imagined part—and processing how imagined experience and real-life communion with Jesus intersect.

For a guided exercise of imagination prayer, designate one person to select and read the passage aloud several times while other members practice steps 5–9 above as individuals. When everyone has found a comfortable posture and position in the room, the leader instructs the group to take several deep breaths in and out together. Ask the Lord to be present.

- Invite the group to listen to the passage, imagining the physical environment. Read the passage aloud the first time at a neutral rate, and wait one minute.

- Then invite the group to imagine the other people in the scene with Jesus. This time read the passage slowly, pausing after each phrase, and then wait in silence for two minute.

- For the third reading, invite the group to place themselves in the scene and imagine what their bodies feel. Read the passage, emphasizing the action words, and wait in silence for four minutes.

- The fourth time, instruct the group to hear what the speakers in the passage are saying, and then read the passage emphasizing the spoken words. Wait in silence for six minutes.

- Finally, tell the group to imagine themselves as one of the characters in the passage. Tell them that when you are done reading, they can freeze frame, stay with a particular picture involving themselves and Jesus, talk to him, listen to what he says, and abide in his presence. Then read the passage in a neutral tone and pause in silence for eight minutes.

Ask the group to fasten in their minds anything that stands out from their conversations or about their experiences. When members have regrouped, invite them to share how they experienced the scene, what their interaction with Jesus was like, and how the imagined encounter might intersect with their current real-world situations. Allow others in the group to ask questions that might provoke thoughtful reflection, but avoid debating whose imagined version was right or accurate.

Whole group imagination prayer requires another level of commitment, since each one must practice both role-playing and self-awareness throughout the exercise. Instead of choosing an action scene with Jesus, find a parable that he told in the gospels, such as the Good Samaritan (Luke 10:25–37). As a group, read the passage and identify key characters and their primary actions. After these details are decided, each member should sit quietly and individually consider which character she identifies with, why she identifies with that character, and how Jesus might call her to fulfill this role in the next few moments. Invite the Lord to reveal his real-life call to individuals through the role-playing to follow.

When everyone is ready, each person modeling a particular character should group themselves together. In the Good Samaritan, for example, all the hurt people should lay down in the middle of the room. All the caregiver innkeepers should wait for a hurt person to be brought to them and then faithfully minister to that person's real-life needs. All the sensitive Samaritans should tend to a hurt person, convey her to the caregiver, and return to check on her.

It is not important that there be equal numbers of each role-player, nor that much acting occur. Indeed, do not allow your concentration on what Jesus might be doing and saying through this exercise of imagination prayer to become distracted by trying to act the part "right" or well. What is important is that each person be present both to the action and to how Jesus is using the role-playing to speak to the real-life needs of group members. Is he inviting a "hurt person" to share a real need with a "Samaritan" or an "inn-keeper," for example? Or is he simply providing the hurt person a ministry to be received?

When all of the members are done, regroup and share how each one experienced the scene and what her interaction with Jesus was like.

Consider

1. Have you ever experienced a long, unavoidable season of pondering like Ignatius' illness or his long journeys? What did you think about? Did you find the lack of diversion beneficial? Tedious? How so?

2. Fully knowing someone involves sharing experience with that person, not just knowing about him or her. What are the advantages to relational knowledge that you cannot get with mere information? What do you risk in knowing Jesus this way? What do you fear Jesus discovering in you?

3. What church traditions in our day emphasize experience and emotions? How is imagination prayer similar to these traditions? Different?

4. Describe the benefits of being tied to a particular passage of Scripture. What are the limits of imagination prayer?

5. Think about praying this prayer in a group. How would it help or hinder for a designated reader to repeat the passage every few minutes? How could members of a group help one another unpack the encounter and relate it back to the *non*-imagined aspects of their lives?

Study Further

Blythe, Theresa A. "Ignatian Imagination Prayer" Pages 100–102 and 188 in *50 Ways to Pray: Practices from Many Traditions and Times*. Nashville, Tenn.: Abingdon, 2006.

Foster, Richard J. "Stretching Out to God." Pages 59–60 in *Prayer: Finding the Heart's True Home*. New York: HarperSanFrancisco, 1992.

Guenther, Margaret. "Ignatian Prayer." Pages 62–63 in *The Practice of Prayer*. Volume 4 in *The New Church's Teaching Series*. Cambridge, Mass.: Cowley, 1998.

Hutchinson, Gloria. "Ignatius of Loyola: The Sensual Christian." Pages 56–80 in *Six Ways to Pray from Six Great Saints*. Cincinnati, Ohio: St. Anthony Messenger, 1982.

"Ignatius of Loyola: Movements Produced in the Soul." Pages 193–99 in *Devotional Classics: Selected Readings for Individuals and Groups, revised and expanded*. Edited by Richard J. Foster and James Bryan Smith. New York: HarperSanFrancisco, 2005.

Mayfield, Sue. "Praying with the Imagination." Pages 108–12 in *Exploring Prayer*. Peabody, Mass.: Hendrickson, 2007.

"An Online Retreat." No pages. Omaha, Nebr.: Collaborative Ministry Office of Creighton University, 1999. Cited 1 Aug 2006. Online: www.creighton.edu/CollaborativeMinistry/cmo-retreat.html.

Rhodes, Tricia McCary. Pages 61–62 in *The Soul at Rest: A Journey into Contemplative Prayer*. Grand Rapids, Mich.: Bethany House, 1996.

Silf, Margaret. "Meeting the Lord in Imaginative Prayer." Pages 210–13 in *Inner Compass: An Invitation to Ignatian Spirituality*. Chicago: Loyola, 1999.

Lectio Divina

BENEDICT'S PRAYER WITH THE SCRIPTURES

Lectio divina is devotional reading of Scripture, followed by meditative consideration of the personal impact of that Scripture, verbal response to the reading and meditation, and contemplative response through active or passive reception.

LECTIO DIVINA ("holy reading"), or reading Scripture with the purpose of grounding our prayers, assumes that conversation with God is not only possible, but eagerly expected by God. In providing us with Scripture, God has spoken his word to us for our time, regardless of whether we are well-educated or illiterate (Heb 4:12). When we listen and respond to the Bible, we seek to know the Word made flesh, who is revealed there[68] (1 John 1:1–2). We actively practice our belief that his Holy Spirit will supply the light that we need to understand and receive the Word (John 16:13). Benedict of Nursia believed this and sought to commune with Christ by first trusting that Christ would make himself known (Jer 29:12–14).

Benedict was born in 480 in the Apennine Mountains of what is now Italy. He came from a good family, who sent him to Rome to study, but the licentious behavior of his fellow students, indeed of the entire crumbling Empire, distressed him. Abandoning the scholastic life, he took to

---

[68] M. Basil Pennington, *Lectio Divina: Renewing the Ancient Practice of Praying the Scriptures* (New York: Crossroad, 1998), 5–6.

the hills to dwell in a cave and to seek Christ as a hermit. Impressed with his devotion, some local monks asked him to become their abbot, which he did reluctantly. However, his governance proved too strict, so they tried to free themselves by poisoning him. The attempt failed to kill him, but it did drive him back to his hermitage.

Nevertheless, his fame continued to spread and others joined him or sent their sons to experience what was then considered the "complete" Christian life: monastic community (Acts 2:44–47). Eventually he established twelve monasteries in the region, each with twelve monks, but his popularity made him the target of local clergy.

At the age of fifty, he left Subiaco and moved halfway to Naples. He and his disciples destroyed the temple of Apollo that they found on Monte Cassino and established a new monastery, where lay people, bishops, and even the king of the Goths sought his counsel. He died (c. 547) shortly after his twin sister, St. Scholastica, who had also followed the monastic way and resided in a convent nearby.[69]

Benedict's enduring contribution is the Rule he developed to guide the monks toward complete devotion and holiness. It outlines times of silence, encourages the monastery to be self-sufficient, and gathers the community in worship and prayer throughout the day. In the forty-eighth chapter of the Rule, Benedict states that community members "should have specified periods for manual labor

---

[69] Timothy Fry, preface to *The Rule of St. Benedict in English,* by Benedict (ed. Timothy Fry; Collegeville, Minn.: Liturgical, 1982), 9–10.

as well as for prayerful reading."[70] He explains this prayerful reading as cultivating the ability to listen deeply, to hear "with the ear of your heart" (prologue 1).[71]

Later, prayerful reading or *lectio divina* was systematized into four steps: reading, meditation, prayer, and contemplation. Reading signified "looking on Holy Scripture with all one's will and wit," what we call Bible study. Meditation meant "a studious insearching with the mind to know what was before concealed"; that is, considering how the Scripture may be speaking to you in particular. Prayer proper involved "a devout desiring of the heart to get what is good and avoid what is evil." This is prayer as we tend to think of it: responding to the Scripture with praise, thanksgiving, confession, or requests. And contemplation concluded the reading with a "lifting up of the heart to God," sometimes through action.[72]

Some of us start with lifting up our hearts and would just as soon end there. Like the Romans of Benedict's time, we know how to celebrate, but the stillness of contemplation sounds tedious at first. Prayerful reading provides a habit for receiving the "whole counsel" of God (Acts 20:27 KJV), so that the life of our party becomes the fullness of Christ's joy (Ps 84:2; John 10:10).

Others of us come to Scripture already in love with its drama and tragedy. *Lectio divina* grounds our imaginations in

---

[70] Benedict, *The Rule of St. Benedict in English* (ed. Timothy Fry; Collegeville, Minn.: Liturgical, 1982), 69.

[71] Ibid., 15.

[72] "Letter of Dom Guigo the Carthusian to Brother Gervase about the Contemplative Life," (ed. Fish Eaters), n.p. [cited 12 Jan 2006]. Online: www.fisheaters.com//guigo.html.

the Word. Not only do we read the word; *lectio* allows Christ the Word to study us in return (John 1:14). As we discipline our hearts to move back into principles of truth, we discover how the Christian story of suffering and glory takes root in reality and practice (Matt 5:16; Jas 2:22).

Still others, like Benedict, are so driven by correct Scripture-interpretation and obedience that we forget to enjoy the process of listening and responding to Jesus and the people in our communities (Jas 1:23–25). Instead we can comfort ourselves and teach others that obedience to Scripture principles will silence the nagging sense that we lack holiness or devotion. The steps of prayerful reading can shift this right thinking out of the mind into the heart and finally into right action (1 John 5:20).

Practice

1. Find a comfortable place to read and pray. You may wish to designate a particular chair or cushion or organize the space with a candle, a picture, or a favorite mug. Over time, these physical modifications to the environment will cue your mind to begin quieting itself for prayer automatically.

2. Choose a passage. Perhaps you will follow the daily office, reading a designated portion from the Psalms, the Old Testament, an epistle, and a gospel each day. You may stick to a reading guide that takes you through the whole Bible in a year. Or you may use a Bible study guide. If the practice of reading the Bible is new for you, start with the story of Jesus in the Gospels of Mark or Luke.

3. Invite the Lord to be present as you read, to illuminate the text so that you understand it (Col 1:9). *Read* the passage several times, looking for literary clues to its meaning. This is time for Bible study. What genre is the writing (for example, is it narrative, instructive, apocalyptic, prophetic, poetic)? What is the larger context of the passage? Who are the characters, the readers, the author? What is the plot? What are the main ideas? How does the logical argument flow? What figures of speech do you find? What questions do you have? You may wish to clarify the passage by using the editor's introduction, study notes, cross references, and concordance that are printed in your Bible, or you can open up Bible reference tools like dictionaries, lexicons, and commentaries to help you grasp the basic ideas. However, do not turn your reading into a critical interpretation project. This is time for devotional reading. Save the deep research for later.

4. Once you have the big picture, *meditate* on the passage, allowing the Word to read you (Ps 19:7). Ask the Lord to guide your thoughts as you consider what he might be saying through this Scripture to you in particular.

Reread the passage several times, listening for words or phrases that speak to you. Some people free-write in a journal at this stage, beginning with the words, phrases, or theological themes of the Scripture that stand out to them. Others doodle to help them concentrate, illustrating what comes to mind from the passage, recreating the words in special font or color, or embellishing the printed text. Or you may simply sit, quietly attending to the direction in your mind.

Stay with a phrase that speaks to you for a while. Wait. Your subconscious mind may grasp something that will take your conscious mind a few moments to "hear" and receive.

Savor the phrase. At this stage, avoid analyzing it. This is like tasting your favorite candy. You do not consider the chemical components and how they react with your taste receptors to sense that it tastes good. You simply enjoy the result.

Be aware of potential distractions running through your mind.

- Are these thoughts tugging you away from the phrase?
    - Is there another word or phrase? You may move on to it in a moment. For now, return to the first phrase.
    - Do you wonder whether you are deceiving yourself? How can you know if God is really communicating with you? Be at peace (Ps 16:11–12). God is not a trickster. He is stronger than your self-deceptive tendencies. You may trust him to reveal what you need to hear without leading you down false paths.
    - Is your mind multitasking while it waits? Jot your "to do" list on a separate piece of paper. You can attend to it in a few minutes.

- Are the thoughts that are running through your mind intersecting with your phrase? Perhaps they are the substance of your meditation rather than a path away from it. God brings your subconscious and your conscious thoughts into the light of his word. You need not protect him from your negative or chaotic ideas. You do not need a finished package before you yield yourself to him.[73]

5. When your engagement with the text has settled, turn to the Lord in *prayer*. Perhaps your reading and meditation will lead you to praise God's character or deeds. Maybe something has come to light that you wish to confess or for which you want to ask forgiveness. Perhaps you will thank him or petition his help in something or for someone. A phrase from the Scriptures you have been reading may provide the right words or you may speak your own. Now is the time to talk with God (1 Cor 14:15).

6. *Contemplation* involves waiting on the truths you have learned about God and about yourself, but it may include active waiting as well as passive. Perhaps a specific effort will be part of the response to your prayerful reading (Jas 1:23–25). You may need to speak to someone or change a habit. Maybe you will start that in-depth Scripture-analysis now. Or you may share with others the themes and thoughts that arose as you read, meditated, and prayed

---

[73] Jesuit Communication Centre, *Sacred Space*, n.p. [cited 13 Jan 2006]. Online: www.sacredspace.ie.

(Heb 10:24–25). On the other hand, waiting might mean centering in stillness, repeating and returning your mind to a word or phrase that captures the truth you received. Finally, you may simply rest, comforted and empowered through the spiritual exercise for the other activities of the day (Ps 119:52).

Sample the Prayer

Lectio divina need not take a long time if you limit your reading, meditation, prayer proper, and contemplation to one verse of Scripture for each day. Daily practice helps maintain the flow of ideas and the momentum. Rereading yesterday's verse quickly reminds you what has already transpired in the passage or in your own response. This may be difficult with narrative books of Scripture such as Chronicles or the Gospels, but it works well with shorter prophetic books such as Amos or teaching books such as James.

Practice Together

Consider practicing *lectio divina* as a small group. Designate one person to select the passage and facilitate the group's study for 10–15 minutes. Once the group understands the passage, get comfortable, close your eyes, and listen as each person takes a turn reading it aloud. Pause for several minutes after each person reads and ponder silently what stood out to you in each one's reading. When the meditation concludes, join one another in spoken prayer. Perhaps you will pray aloud spontaneously in short bursts, sometimes called "popcorn prayer." Or perhaps you will pray the Lord's Prayer in unison or the suffrages responsively (see pp 84–85). Whatever your practice, do not rush, but allow yourselves to be led by the voices around you. Finally, take time to talk about what themes seemed to sound throughout the group, what "word" the group can take away, or what words to individuals have arisen during your group *lectio*.

Consider

1. Have you ever taken a spiritual retreat alone or with your community? What are the advantages of seeking God in a special time of seclusion away from regular life? What may be the benefits of a hermitage or a monastic setting for regular life instead of a short retreat? How would it help one's prayer life to become complete, holy, and/or devoted? What may be the drawbacks?

2. Doodling and free-writing help focus attention during meditation. Why do you suppose these techniques aid in moving the knowledge you gain from reading into the arena of experience? How else do they change the nature of your meditation? What other tools might you use to aid in waiting on the Scripture?

3. How does the prayer step of *lectio divina* compare with your more spontaneous prayers? How might beginning with Scripture rather than starting with your particular circumstances change the nature of your prayers?

4. What are some advantages of *lectio divina's* heavy structure? How do you feel about starting with understanding

instead of imagination? Do you come away with a different perspective than you started with?

5. How do you think holy reading differs when practiced as a group rather than alone? What inhibits or assists the group in fostering intimacy and trust for this sort of practice? Was it easier for you to concentrate, to hear something during *lectio divina* with the group or alone? Often in holy-reading instructions for groups, the prayer step is omitted. Why might it be important to retain that step before sharing, even though praying aloud to God can be more challenging for some than sharing with other people?

Study Further

Bible Gateway. No pages. Muskegon, Mich.: Gospel Communications International, 2006. Noted 13 January 2006. Online: www.biblegateway.com.

Blue Letter Bible. No pages. Noted 13 January 2006. Online: www .blueletterbible.org.

Blythe, Theresa A. "Lectio Divina." Pages 46–48 and 161–63 in *50 Ways to Pray: Practices from Many Traditions and Times.* Nashville, Tenn.: Abingdon, 2006.

Foster, Richard J. "Meditative Prayer." Pages 143–54 in *Prayer: Finding the Heart's True Home.* New York: HarperSanFrancisco, 1992.

Guenther, Margaret. "Lectio Divina." Pages 67–69 in *The Practice of Prayer.* Volume 4 in *The New Church's Teaching Series.* Cambridge, Mass.: Cowley, 1998.

Harrington, Daniel J. "Lectio Divina: Contemporary Catholics on Traditional Devotions." *America* 188 (31 March 2003), n.p. Noted 12 January 2006. Online: www.americamagazine.org/gettext.cfm?articleTypeID=1&t extID=2886&issueID=428#.

Mayfield, Sue. Pages 37–38 and 104–6 in *Exploring Prayer*. Peabody, Mass.: Hendrickson, 2007.

Sacred Space. No pages. Dublin: Jesuit Communication Centre, 1999. Cited 13 Jan 2006. Online: www.sacred space.ie.

Rhodes, Tricia McCary. Pages 25, 28, and 104 in *The Soul at Rest: A Journey into Contemplative Prayer*. Grand Rapids, Mich.: Bethany House, 1996.

The Rule of St. Benedict in English. Edited by Timothy Fry, OSB. Collegeville, Minn.: Liturgical, 1982.

Thurston, Bonnie. "Praying the Word: *Lectio Divina*." Pages 54–68 in *For God Alone: A Primer on Prayer*. Notre Dame, Ind.: University of Notre Dame Press, 2009.

Wolpert, Daniel. "Journaling: Writing What God Shows Us." Pages 101–112 and 183–84 in *Creating a Life with God: The Call of Ancient Prayer Practices*. Nashville, Tenn.: Upper Room, 2003.

Wolpert, Daniel. "Lectio Divina: Encountering Scripture through Sacred Reading." Pages 37–49 and 175–77 in *Creating a Life with God: The Call of Ancient Prayer Practices*. Nashville, Tenn.: Upper Room, 2003.

Body Prayer

Gregory of Nyssa's Physical Faith

Body prayer is physical activity that promotes spiritual communion with God, sometimes accompanied by verbal communication, but often simply experienced as spending time doing something together with him.

Participating physically in prayer changes the nature of our conversations with God. For some, action prayer adds dimension to what would otherwise feel like flat words (Matt 6:7). For others, engaging the body frees us from the tyranny of the mind so that we can listen to the Lord's voice, not just our own (Isa 50:5). Many of the writings of the Cappadocian fathers wrestled with just exactly how this body participation in communion with God worked.

These three church fathers were born early in the fourth century in a region called Cappadocia, near modern-day Armenia. Two of them attended school together and grew up to be known as Basil the Great and Gregory of Nazianzus.

The third, Basil's younger brother, also named Gregory (of Nyssa, c. 335–c. 394), did not want to be a professional churchman. He had neither Basil's administrative skills, nor the other Gregory's eloquence in preaching. Instead, he used his education to become a lawyer. Big brother Basil did not approve. To force him out of the secular job, he appointed Gregory bishop of Nyssa. Gregory could not resist. As a bishop, he continued to exert his keen mind, however, and eventually became the most proficient writer and theologian of the three.

For many years, the trio corresponded regularly. When the larger church fought over whether Jesus was spirit or flesh, the three men took up the discussion of this paradox in their letters (John 1:14; 4:24). Together they reasoned that Jesus was the same divine substance or essence as the Father—nothing less (John 10:30)—but also that Jesus was human—and thus unique. They argued for three distinct, yet permanently cooperating, persons or "faces" of one God: Father, Son, and Holy Spirit (Rom 1:1–4). It is this tri-unity understanding that comes down to us in the Nicene Creed.

In 381, Gregory presented their Trinity concept to a gathering of church leaders at the Second Ecumenical Council, where he lobbied strongly for its adoption. After the council, he traveled to Syria, Arabia, and Jerusalem, helping churches resolve their sometimes bloody disunity over the issue by offering believers the option that Jesus was one whole—both "very divine" *and* "very human."

Gregory was the first writer to link Christ's act of becoming human to save humans with Christians' acts of eating and drinking communion and getting wet in baptism (1 Cor 11:26; Heb 10:22). He wrote that receiving these physical sacraments played a role in a person's spiritual cooperation with God: "Since the method of our salvation was made effectual, not so much by [Christ's] precepts, . . . as by [his] deeds, . . . it was necessary that some means should be devised by which there might be . . . a kind of affinity and likeness between him who follows and him who leads the way."[74]

Spiritual gifts did not work apart from observable fruits of this cooperation.[75] Prophecy, for example, was a useless gift if it was not physically practiced with love and did not bear the fruit of love (1 Cor 13:8–9; Gal 5:22–23). More than any other writer of his time, Gregory articulated the association: physical signs of faith both point to and participate in mysteries of faith.

Fourth century controversies were not the last conflicts to arise over how one's body engages one's redemption. Today, you still cannot attend church for very long before you hear such questions. What is the exact nature of the bread and wine with regard to Jesus' body and blood? Is sprinkling sufficient for baptism, or must you be fully immersed? Shall we raise hands and dance or keep silence in worship? Will we recite ancient prayers or speak in spiritual tongues? The fact is we do not fully comprehend how the body-spirit mystery works, so we discuss it . . . a lot.

What we do know is that you do not *have* a body; you *are* a body just as much as you are a mind and a spirit.[76] Modern learning theories and brain science support this

---

[74] Gregory of Nyssa, *The Great Catechism* 37 (vol. 5 of *The Nicene and Post-Nicene Fathers;* Series 2; ed. Philip Schaff and Henry Wace; 1886–1889; 14 vols.; repr. Peabody, Mass.: Hendrickson, 1994), 502.

[75] Stanley M. Burgess, *The Holy Spirit: Ancient Christian Traditions* (Peabody, Mass.: Hendrickson, 1984), 144–51.

[76] Richard J. Foster, *Prayer: Finding the Heart's True Home* (New York: HarperSanFrancisco, 1992), 116.

scriptural assumption. Multiple-intelligence studies suggest that human understanding grows by doodling and tasting, as well as by reading and taking notes.[77] And left brain/right brain studies indicate that the right hemisphere, the faith and religion side, needs more exercise.[78]

Many religions encourage such exercises as burning incense, lighting candles, walking the labyrinth, tracing mandalas, dancing, and looking at icons because they know that engaging the whole person in worship is powerful. Some of these methods are used by Christians, too. Long before Gregory, the psalmist urged worshipers to "Lift up your hands to the holy place and bless the Lord!" (Ps 134:2 RSV) and implored God to "Let my prayer be counted as incense before thee" (Ps 141:2 RSV). Your body's posture, your speech, your song, your hearing, your senses of smell and taste, and your hand motions change how you listen to the Lord and how you respond.

Body prayer taps our right-brain listening tools of dimension, imagination, and faith and momentarily sets aside our left-brain demands for black and white, yes or no answers. Instead of worries and wants encumbering the mind, shapes, sounds, and motions occupy it, allowing deeper longings to rise up and be addressed (Ps 42:2). In addition to telling God what is on our prayer list, employing our whole bodies creates space for prayer to

---

[77] Neil D. Fleming and Charles C. Bonwell, "VARK: A Guide to Learning Styles," n.p. [cited 11 Jan 2006]. Online: www.vark-learn.com/english/index.asp.

[78] Dan Eden, "Left Brain: Right Brain," n.p. [cited 11 Jan 2006]. Online: www.viewzone.com/bicam.html.

become a communion of trust.

Sharing a prayer activity with the Father—rather than simply listing our expectations of him, ourselves, and others—feels more like breaking bread together than flying in for a business lunch (Exod 17:7; Luke 22:15). We relax our need for an immediate word of affirmation, and this allows a sense of God's intimate presence to sneak in through the back door of action and artistic play. Body prayer allows us to enjoy our time with the Lord. And it is this communion that satisfies our hearts.

Practice

1. Choose an activity that you will dedicate to body prayer. With a little research, you can pursue ancient prayer arts like walking the labyrinth. Others might designate a modern activity, such as shooting hoops or cross-stitching, for body prayer. Perhaps you would prefer to commandeer a daily chore like walking the dog. Or you might want to dip into your brain's artistic side by doodling abstractly or coloring a book of geometric shapes.

2. Find any equipment you need (the dog's leash, colored pencils and paper, etc.) and a location where you won't be disturbed by interested observers. You may load your headset with modern worship songs, recorded Scripture, or classical church music to help you focus. Or you may choose the stillness of silence.

3. Turn off your phone, pager, social networking site, email, etc. Quiet yourself before the Lord and invite him into your

prayer time. Ask him to direct and protect your thoughts from foolishness and deception. You may suggest a topic of conversation with him, perhaps a choice you have to make or a tricky relationship or an unhealthy attitude. You may ask him to bring something to mind. Or you may simply decide to be together without a specific agenda.

4. Whatever the activity you choose, the goal is to free your mind from immediate concerns by using a single, repetitive motion to focus your attention. This activity is different than an intercessory prayer walk, where you make requests for the neighborhood as you circle the local buildings, or an artistic expression, which depicts visually or audibly how you feel. Ironically, the purpose of body prayer is to limit yourself to a single activity as a means of stilling yourself to listen to God's voice (Ps 46:10).

5. When you are ready, turn on your headset and begin. Allow yourself to wander wherever the dog leads or to doodle freeform, for example. Do not obsess with accuracy, precision, or perfect pace. Enjoy the mix of colors, shapes, and movement that you encounter. Trusting the Lord to reveal what he wishes, let your thoughts roam.

6. Set yourself a time limit and faithfully stop when it is up. You can return to the exercise of prayer tomorrow.

7. Immediately, make a note to yourself of any specific patterns or directions your thoughts took. What did you hear in the worship or in the Scripture that bears more

attention? What issue from your current circumstances dominated? Do you feel like laughing? Are you sad? If you noticed a new thought or synthesis, if you understood an anxiety, if you felt a conclusion emerge, write that down, too. If nothing happened, ask yourself what nothing felt like. Where did you and the dog end up? What shape did nothing take on your paper?

8. Offer your wandering, your notes, your ideas, your feelings to God. Thank him for his guidance, safe-keeping, and peace. If nothing did happen, offer that nothingness to God, thanking him for the chance to be still in his presence (Ps 23:2–3).

9. It may take some time for you to release yourself from expectations of production or success. Often, people become discouraged because they cannot see immediate purpose or meaning in their wanderings, whether by foot or by hand. Western society and sometimes our personalities have conditioned us to trust only the scientific approach of our left brains. Give yourself permission and several chances to simply delight in the right brain artistic "mess" you and God make because you have made it together. Allow yourself to take walks with God that assert no more agenda than spending time together.

Sample the Prayer

If you only have five uninterrupted minutes to spend with God, take note of your posture. Are your arms crossed or open? Are your hands clenched together or relaxed? Are your shoulders tensed or at rest? Are your legs crossed or are your feet planted on the floor? What does your body language tell you (and God) about how you are feeling or what you are thinking at the moment? You have expressed this through your physical position; can you tell God about it with your words, too?

During another five-minute prayer time, simply change your posture. Kneel at your chair or bed instead of sitting. Prostrate yourself on the carpet instead of kneeling. Open your palms and lay them face-up on your lap instead of clasping them together. Look at a picture of Jesus instead of closing your eyes.

Practice Together

If you practice this exercise as a small group or with a friend, take turns suggesting a topic to intersect with your activity. You may also take turns selecting the music or Scripture to which you all listen. When the designated time has elapsed, give yourselves a short period to consider the individual patterns your prayer has followed before sharing these with the group. Some spiritual direction groups choose different media for this exercise; depending on the availability, you might rather sculpt clay, paint, glue pieces of colored paper or found objects into a collage, or walk a labyrinth.

Alternatively, your group may wish to contribute to one canvass, one sculpture, one drawing, or one collage during the designated time frame. You may choose to walk the labyrinth in twos instead of one-by-one. When your activity is complete, you will be able to share, not only individual themes that arose as part of your prayer, but how those themes shifted with the physical interaction of other group members. Furthermore, you may be able to discern what the group's melded prayer seemed to be and to listen for how God would speak to you as a unified community.

Consider

1. Jesus' wholly divine and wholly human nature constitutes one of the most difficult paradoxes of the Christian faith. Believers and seekers alike struggle with it. How does your own fully spiritual and fully physical nature influence the way you understand Jesus? How do these paradoxes influence your relationship with God?

2. Recall a time when something you did or felt physically changed your mind, messed with your emotions, and/or affected your sense of connection with God or others. Considering the impact, what are ways that you already harness the power of your body to influence the state of your spirit? How might you apply these to your personal or corporate prayer life?

3. History has long connected the friendships (and frustrations) of the three Cappadocian church fathers with our three-in-one understanding of God, which grew out of their relationship. How do the interactions of your friends, family, or faith community reflect the interaction of the persons of the Trinity? How, for example, is physical prayer with your group or a friend different than doing this alone?

Do you feel more self-conscious or find it easier to let go of your expectations when you are alone or when you are with a group?

4. If you have tried several types of sacred music or Scripture for this exercise, how do the various pieces flavor your listening? How does the location, lighting, or physical medium change your experience with God?

5. What other activities might lend themselves to body prayer? Which activities do you prefer? Why? Which seem inefficient, goofy, dangerous, or otherwise unappealing to you? What might be the advantages and disadvantages of trying one of those?

Study Further

Blythe, Theresa A. Pages 40–42, 85–97, 159, and 181–87 in *50 Ways to Pray: Practices from Many Traditions and Times.* Nashville, Tenn.: Abingdon, 2006.

✓ Foster, Richard J. "Body Prayer." Pages 116–18 in *Prayer: Finding the Heart's True Home.* New York: HarperSan-Francisco, 1992.

Guenther, Margaret. "Praying with Our Hands." Pages 78–80 in *The Practice of Prayer.* Volume 4 in *The New Church's Teaching Series.* Cambridge, Mass.: Cowley, 1998.

Mayfield, Sue. Pages 17, 70–71, 84–86, and 111–17 in *Exploring Prayer.* Peabody, Mass.: Hendrickson, 2007.

Pagitt, Doug, and Kathryn Prill. *BodyPrayer: The Posture of Intimacy with God.* Illustrated by Colleen Shealer Olson. Colorado Springs, Colo.: WaterBrook, 2005.

Thurston, Bonnie. "Praying with the Body: Some Exercises." Pages 105–127 in *For God Alone: A Primer on Prayer*. Notre Dame, Ind.: University of Notre Dame Press, 2009.

Thurston, Bonnie. "Prayer: Toward an Anthropology." Pages 69–85 in *For God Alone: A Primer on Prayer*. Notre Dame, Ind.: University of Notre Dame Press, 2009.

Wolpert, Daniel. "Creativity and the Divine: To Create Is to Pray." Pages 89–100 and 182–83 in *Creating a Life with God: The Call of Ancient Prayer Practices*. Nashville, Tenn.: Upper Room, 2003.

Wolpert, Daniel. "Walking Toward God: The Journey Made Visible." Pages 125–35 and 185–86 in *Creating a Life with God: The Call of Ancient Prayer Practices*. Nashville, Tenn.: Upper Room, 2003.

Appendix
QUICK REFERENCE SUMMARIES OF EACH
PRAYER PRACTICE

Breath Prayer

1. Sit comfortably with your back straight and close your eyes.
2. Pay attention to your breathing.
3. Ask Jesus to be present, to guide, protect, and draw you into the communion of the Trinity.
4. Wait silently until you feel ready to begin praying.
5. Pray in your breathing rhythm.
   - Inhale: Lord, Jesus Christ,
   - Pause: Son of God,
   - Exhale: have mercy on me, a sinner.
6. Repeat the breath prayer ten times.
7. Pause, telling Christ about what has risen to your mind.
8. Begin the next ten when you are ready.
9. Continue the cycles of prayer and pause until the silence is gathered.
10. Write down anything that particularly stood out to you.

Music Prayer

1. Find a piece of music that moves you.
2. Consider what the lyrics mean to you. How do they express your thoughts to God?
3. Pray the words aloud (in English) without the music, listening to the meaning they evoke.
4. Listen to the music again, attending to the words and noticing your physical response.

___en to the piece again, resisting the urge to pick out specific words, instruments, or rhythms.

6. Listen a third time, allowing the music and your response to speak to God.

7. Write down or share with a friend how the music and your own thoughts intersected.

Action Prayer

1. As you pass through your day, yield to God the tasks that you do and the reactions that you feel.

2. Offer your attitude honestly. Then *act* as Jesus has asked.

3. Do not lose the language of action just because words are available.

4. When you forget or fail, remember that God rejoices at your desire to share his work.

5. At the end of the day, record what you learned or received.

6. Return to the Scripture and perhaps to verbal prayer.

Presence Prayer

1. Invite the Lord to rule your day before you rise and offer him the results before you fall asleep.

2. Designate several days or weeks to practice this way. Then note down anything that has changed.

3. Choose something regular in your day to prompt you to pause and invite the Lord in.

4. Regularly note the impact that these rest-stops have in your ordinary life.

5. See how many minutes in a day you can be aware of God's presence.

6. Pick one hour each day to continuously cooperate with God, even in the littlest tasks.

7. If other people distract you, pray for them in a small shift of awareness.

8. Address God in the second person instead of trying to concentrate on an abstract idea of deity.

9. Let go of perceived failures and begin again with a clean slate at any instant.

Extemporaneous Prayer

1. Speak to God as though he is sitting next to you; tell him what is on your mind.

2. Start now. Do not put it off until everything is in order. There is no need to prepare.

3. Be honest with God because he sees and receives you just as you are.

4. Follow a guide such as the ACTS acronym if you need a prompt. *Adoration, Confession, Thanksgiving, Supplication*

5. Offer God issues outside yourself.

6. Tell him what you long for.

7. When you are finished, wait for a moment. Allow God to respond.

8. Make a written note of how your conversation progressed.

9. Keep yourself on track by scheduling your time with God into a date book or PDA.

Prayer of Examen

1. Choose a piece of Scripture to act as a mirror for your soul.

2. Ask God for insight into how the truth in Scripture and your own experience have intersected.

3. Read slowly, pausing at each sentence or verse to listen for anything that stands out.

4. If you find your mind wandering, move on to the next sentence or verse.

5. Avoid the urge to defend or to punish yourself. Trust that you will receive God's mercy.

6. Thank God for evidence of his work through you.

7. If it is difficult to hear his voice about your life, listen for *his* characteristics or actions instead.

8. Write down your confession to God, both the truth about yourself and the truth about him.

9. Do not forget that when you leave the mirror, you can leave with confidence and peace.

Liturgical Prayer

1. Choose a liturgical prayer to practice.

2. Read the words of the written prayer to yourself slowly. Do not skim.

3. Mouth the prayer to yourself or whisper it softly.

4. Pray the prayer out loud. Resist the temptation to race or to focus on correct emphasis.

5. Pause in silence as the ring of the prayer settles.

6. Repeat the prayer again. This time focus on the Lord before whom you offer these words.

7. At the "Amen," pause again to listen.

8. Write down the aspects of the prayer or the praying that spoke for you or your community today.

9. Notice the words of the prayer returning to you throughout the day.

Imagination Prayer

1. Pick an action scene from the gospels as a foundation for your prayer.

2. Read the passage several times.

3. Invite the Lord to be present with you, to guide and protect as you seek to be with him.

4. Now quiet yourself before God.

5. Let your imagination work on the gospel scene.

- Imagine the location.
- What time of day is it?
- See the people involved.
- How do your feet feel?
- What do you smell?
- What do you taste?
- What is being said by Jesus and others?
- What actions are taken by Jesus and others?

6. Take the place of one of the characters and see the scene through the eyes of that person.

7. Release your imagination from your inner critic.

8. Choose to be "taken in" by your encounter with Jesus without being sucked under by the scene.

9. Stay with a particular picture involving yourself and Jesus. Talk to him and listen to what he says.

10. Write down what you have heard, what happened, what you said, or what the themes were.

Lectio Divina

1. Find a comfortable place to read and pray.

2. Choose a passage.

3. Invite the Lord to be present as you read, to illuminate the text so that you understand it.

4. *Read* the passage several times, looking for literary clues to its meaning.

5. Ask the Lord to guide your thoughts as you consider what he might be saying to you in particular.

6. Reread the passage, listening for words or phrases that speak to you.

7. When your engagement with the text has settled, respond to God with requests, praise, etc.

6. Wait on the truths you have learned in passive and/or active reception.

Body Prayer

1. Choose an activity that you will dedicate to body prayer.

2. Find any equipment you need and a location where you will not be disturbed.

3. Turn off your phone, social networking site, etc. Quiet yourself and invite God into your prayer.

4. Limit yourself to a single activity as a means of stilling yourself to listen to God's voice.

5. Do not obsess with precision. Trusting the Lord to reveal what he wishes, let your thoughts roam.

6. Set yourself a time limit and faithfully stop when it is up.

7. Immediately, make a note to yourself of any specific patterns or directions your thoughts took.

8. Offer your wandering, your notes, your ideas, your feelings to God.

9. Give yourself permission to simply delight in spending time with God this way.

About the Author

Dawn Duncan Harrell, MDiv, has served as a spiritual director, teacher, and lecturer on prayer at Park Street Church and Boston Rescue Mission, in Boston, Massachusetts. She is former associate editor of church history, Gospels, and practical theology for Hendrickson Publishers. Now while her daughter plays at preschool, she continues to write and ministers in a lay capacity at Colonial Church in Edina, Minnesota.

Follow her at twitter.com/dwndncnhrrll.
Contact her at dawnduncanharrell.com.
Read about her prayer adventures at tenwaystopray.com.
Write about your own experiences with these prayers at www.facebook.com/tenwaystopray.

Grannon's
Swensons
Mario + Me
La Portes al + Paula